Their Own Dear Days

Supplement to
Where Elm Trees Grew
Fiddleford in Dorset

Olive A. Hall

Typeset and printed in England by
Creeds the Printers, Broadoak, Bridport, Dorset.

ISBN 0 9513372 1 1

ACKNOWLEDGEMENTS

I would like to thank the following for supplying photographs and documents, and in several instances for providing information and writing accounts of their own and their families' recollections and accomplishments.

Anne Barnes
Isobel Bretherton
Dorothy Byrne
Fred Corbin
Kathleen Crew
Averil, Hilda & Victor Cross
H. L. Douch
Evelyn Fellowes Andrews
Gordon Francis
Joan Goodwin
Connie Guttridge
W. A. Haskell
John Illingworth
Barbara Lamble
Iris Loder

Alister Matheson
Olive Matheson
Jim Oliver
Robin Rendell
Nellie Ridout
Gwyn Rogers
Stella Rose
Betty Savage
Ruth Sawley
Geoffrey Tapper
Irene Thomas
Kenneth Topp
Vera Upshall
M. O. Welch
David Wright

the Archivist and Staff at the Dorset County Records Office, Dorchester

and most of all, my husband Ray, without whose understanding and encouragement I should not have completed this book.

CONTENTS

FOREWORD

When Where Elm Trees Grew was published in 1988 I had no idea that it would arouse so much interest locally, in other parts of the country, and as far afield as Europe, Canada, the United States of America, Australia and New Zealand. A number of people were enthusiastic enough to write to me with their personal or their parents' memories of Fiddleford, and some sent the results of their own research, with photographs and copies of documents.

It seemed a pity to file this away unseen by all but me and I therefore decided to record it, if only for the benefit of future generations. In several cases the text is published exactly as it was received from my correspondents, as personal memories are best conveyed in the writer's own words.

Of course, I did further research of my own, adding to what in 1988 I thought was more or less everything which could be discovered about Fiddleford! During the past four years there have been changes to some of the properties in the hamlet, and the 1891 Census Returns are now available to the public.

Their Own Dear Days may appear unbalanced and disjointed — this is because some correspondents supplied a considerable amount of fresh information, whilst few or no new facts came to light about other people or properties mentioned in Where Elm Trees Grew. I felt that even the smallest item was worthy of inclusion, as it might prove to be the 'missing link' for some future researcher.

It is surprising to discover that, although Fiddleford is such a tiny community, descendants of the folk who lived there in the 18th and 19th centuries have settled in many parts of the world. It may be of interest to read of their accomplishments in these distant places, and from the photographs to picture some of those who were previously familiar only by name.

I hope that this second small volume will complement its predecessor and give some pleasure to everyone who is interested in Fiddleford past and present.

Olive A. Hall
1992

ABBREVIATIONS

The following abbreviations have been used:
D.C.R.O.   Dorset County Records Office
P.R.O.   Public Records Office
S.C.R.O.   Suffolk County Records Office
W.E.T.G.   Where Elm Trees Grew

In family charts   —   b baptised   c christened   b.c. baptised circa
    B buried   d died   m married   S.N. Sturminster Newton

In census returns   —   ag. lab. agricultural labourer

Items in small print and square brackets [ ] author's notes

CORRECTIONS

Although the contents of Where Elm Trees Grew were carefully checked before publication, two errors have since come to light. These are given below, with the page numbers in Where Elm Trees Grew:

Page 42, last paragraph.
"(two mills means two mill-wheels)" should read "(two mills means two mill-stones)".

Page 196, 3rd paragraph.
Thomas Hilliar, who went to evening school at Wistaria Cottage, was the father, not the grandfather, of Mrs. Bert Ridout (nee Nellie Hilliar).

THE MILL HOUSE

BRIDGET PITT OF STRATFIELD SAYE

The information given in paragraph 1 on Page 38 of Where Elm Trees Grew — i.e. *"John Freke Esq. of Hinton St. Mary married Bridget Pitt of Stratfield Saye sometime between 1714 and 1729"* — is as shown in the index to the Pitt-Rivers papers at the D.C.R.O. In the Registers of St. Mary's Church, Sturminster Newton, a marriage is recorded on 4 May 1726 between John Freke and Mrs. Biddy Pitt. Bridget was, in fact, the daughter of the Reverend John Pitt, vicar of Hilton, Dorset. The entry in the Register of Baptisms reads *"Bridgett, daughter of John Pitt, Vicar of Hilton was born ye 11 of August about 9 in ye morning, and was Christened ye 13 September following in ye year of our Lord 1697"*. In the Rev. John Pitt's will, one of the trustees is his daughter, Bridgett Freke. What is the connection with Stratfield Saye?

Hutchins History of Dorset, Vol. 4, Page 87 (3rd edition) shows:

"John Freke Esq.   m.   *Bridget Pitt*
born 1698   *of Stratfieldsay*
buried at Hinton St. Mary 20.9.1761

Shroton.   6 Eliz. the manor was granted to Robert Freke and John Walker by rent of 10s yearly, value £37.18.8.   Freke died seised of it 55 Eliz.   The Frekes seem to have sprung originally from Thorncombe, co. Devon.   Thomas Freke, who died in 1698 without issue, left his estate to Thomas Pile of Baverstock, co. Wilts., esq. and Elizabeth, wife of Thomas Freke of Hannington, for their lives, the reversion to George Pitt of Stratfield Say, esq., to whom on the death of Mr. Pile 1712 and Mr. Freke in 1714, the estate came, and in this family still remains, belonging in 1871 to Lord Rivers."

FIDDLEFORD MILL

ROBERT PITT

Until recently, very little information was available about Robert Pitt, who had tenancy of the mill for six years.

A lease dated 22 September 1779 granted him *"all those two water corn mills called Fiddleford Mills"* [two water mills means two mill stones] on condition that he *"put the Mill in good and tenantable repair"* within two years. [D.C.R.O. D.PIT/T620]

However, it appears that he was unable to fulfil the condition that he must restore the mill building, and he was obliged to leave in 1785, surrendering the lease to John Newman, who, it seems, was prepared to rebuild the mill *"at his own costs and charges"*. Perhaps John Newman (then *"about thirty-four years old"*) was related to the John Newman who apparently held the lease of Sturminster Town Mill in 1762, when he is referred to in the List of Law-day Silver due for payment. The item appears in the Sturminster Newton Court Book [D.C.R.O. D.PIT/M71] and reads: *"Town Mills (John Newman) this paymt Disputed o.o.6"* [6d=2½p]

The document terminating Robert Pitt's lease of Fiddleford Mill includes the rather tragic explanation that *"the said Mills and Premises being now very ruinous and out of repair and the said Robert Pitt not being able to repair and keep up the same owing to his distressed circumstances hath agreed absolutely to sell and assign over the same unto the said John Newman . . . "* [D.C.R.O. D.PIT/T620]

This suggestion that Robert was virtually penniless conjures up visions of a poor labourer, with a wife and growing family to support, struggling to earn a living and eventually having to forfeit all he had worked for in the face of adverse circumstances.

However, this picture is not necessarily an accurate one. In the 1766 Lease for the cottage known as The Trout Alehouse, he was described as *"yeoman"*. A yeoman was a small landowner, usually of middle class. Correspondence and photographs from

Robert Pitt of Belchalwell . . . 1734-1787
(portrait painted 1780)

Barbara Lamble of Sydney, Australia, help to build a picture of a man with certain assets of his own, but with a lifestyle which exceeded his means.

This may not have been the only reason for his failure to maintain the mill. It is possible that he suffered from ill health towards the end of his life. Mrs. Lamble remarked on the difference between two signatures, one in a bold hand on a document dated 1779, and the second in 1785 (when he surrendered the lease of the mill) which was shaky and resembled that of an old man, although he was then only fifty years of age. He died two years later.

Of course, he may also have lacked the necessary business acumen to make a success of his affairs. Whatever the reason, he died in poverty.

Mrs. Lamble, some of whose ancestors (Belbin, Pitt and Matcham) lived in Fiddleford, has for years been tracing her family line, and in 1984 came to Dorchester. She spent a month at the County Records Office, and parts of this chapter comprise the results of her work there and the research she has carried out subsequently.

She says of her great-great-great-grandfather Robert Pitt "His insolvency is no surprise to his descendants — his reputation being of a man who liked the good things of life. His grandson wrote that Robert's wife was left three different small estates by her Matcham aunts and her husband 'managed to get rid of them'. After his death his wife lived 'rent free on the bounty of Lord Rivers' [estate records]. Fortunately Robert's wife, Mary nee Matcham, of a Child Okeford family, was a strong, steady woman who migrated to New South Wales in 1801 with her five surviving children. They did well in Australia."

The drawing reproduced on page 12 is a copy of a portrait of Robert Pitt, painted in 1780. The portrait went to Australia with Robert's widow, Mary, in 1801.

It was being taken back to England in 1859 by a grandson to help trace the family's origins. Tragically the ship, Royal Charter, was

13

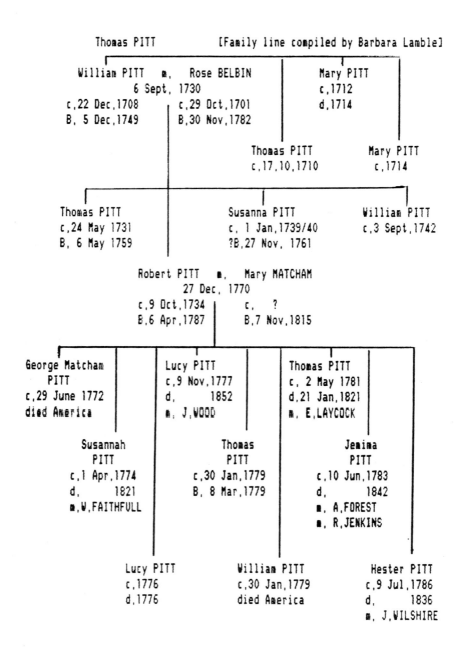

Thomas PITT   [Family line compiled by Barbara Lamble]

William PITT m, Rose BELBIN
6 Sept, 1730
c,22 Dec,1708 c,29 Oct,1701
B, 5 Dec,1749 B,30 Nov,1782

Mary PITT
c,1712
d,1714

Thomas PITT
c,17,10,1710

Mary PITT
c,1714

Thomas PITT
c,24 May 1731
B, 6 May 1759

Susanna PITT
c, 1 Jan,1739/40
?B,27 Nov, 1761

William PITT
c,3 Sept,1742

Robert PITT m, Mary MATCHAM
27 Dec, 1770
c,9 Oct,1734 c, ?
B,6 Apr,1787 B,7 Nov,1815

George Matcham
PITT
c,29 June 1772
died America

Lucy PITT
c,9 Nov,1777
d,   1852
m, J,WOOD

Thomas PITT
c, 2 May 1781
d,21 Jan,1821
m, E,LAYCOCK

Susannah
PITT
c,1 Apr,1774
d,   1821
m,W,FAITHFULL

Thomas
PITT
c,30 Jan,1779
B, 8 Mar,1779

Jemima
PITT
c,10 Jun,1783
d,   1842
m, A,FOREST
m, R,JENKINS

Lucy PITT
c,1776
d,1776

William PITT
c,30 Jan,1779
died America

Hester PITT
c,9 Jul,1786
d,   1836
m, J,WILSHIRE

14

wrecked off Anglesey, Wales. The grandson, his wife and five young sons on their way to school were lost, as was the portrait.

Fortunately a Wilshire grandson of Robert's youngest daughter, Hester Wilshire (nee Pitt), made a black and white drawing of the portrait before it left for England. This drawing is now in the Mitchell Library (the Australian section of the New South Wales State Library).

In 1730, at Sturminster Newton, William, eldest son of Thomas Pitt, married Rose, fifth of eight children born to Benjamin (a miller) and Elizabeth Belbin.

In 1731, William is registered in the estate records as a member of the 'Homage' or jury of the Manor Court. From 1732-1737 he was *"bayliffe of the Hundred and Manor of Sturminster Newton Castle"*. He was also, in 1733, *"Hayward for all the lanes"* and from 1733-1735 *"Assizer of bread and beer"*.

An entry for 1737 reads as follows: *"Item They present John Tapper and Edward Loyte to find a tythingman for Colber Tything for the year ensuing who brought Wm Pitt into Court as their Deputy to Undertake the said Office who was sworn accordingly"*. [D.C.R.O. D.PIT/M69]

Another Minute, recorded in the court proceedings dated 21 October 1737, reads *"The Jury aforesaid upon their Oaths do present and nominate Constables for Sturminster Newton Castle part of the said Hundred, Wm. Heale, Wm. Hassell(?) and John Thring of whom Wm. Heale was elected but he appearing in Court desired Wm. Pitt as his Deputy might be sworn Constable accordingly for the ensueing year"*. [D.C.R.O. D.PIT/M69]

Thomas Pitt (presumably William's eldest son who died in 1759) was bailiff 1752-1759.

The Manor Court, an assembly of tenants presided over by the lord of the manor or his steward, met periodically. The tenants' rights, and those of the lord, were established at the Court Baron. It was here that disputes between tenants were considered and leasehold transfers ratified.

All tenants were obliged to attend the Court Leet, where the jury and other officials were elected. A fine was imposed on anyone who refused to serve. It was here that matters concerning law and order, such as disturbing the peace, were considered.

The *"bayliffe of the Hundred"* was an agent for the lord of the manor, and acted on his behalf in matters concerning the estate. He also supervised demesne land, i.e. the land and/or rights reserved for the lord himself. A typical incident was recorded in court proceedings 21 October 1737 — *"They present Wm. Northover, John Cull, Henry Bartlett, Robt. Lush and Thos Rose for Inclosing part of the Common within this Mannor is therefore ordered that the severall Incrochments by them made be thrown open by the said William Pitt Bayliff and those Haywards hereinbefore mentioned to be sworn for the Commons without Delay."*

The bailiff, on instructions from the lord of the manor or his steward, was responsible for convening the Court. The following notice was issued in 1807:

Hundred and Manor of Sturminster Newton Castle

To the Bailiff of the said Hundred and Manor

You are to give Notice that the Court Leet and Court Baron of the said Hundred and Manor, will be held on Wednesday the Twenty First day of October Instant at Eleven of the Clock in the forenoon at the usual place, and you are to warn all the Officers, Freeholders, Tenants, and Resiants [sic] of an [sic] in the said Hundred and Manor, to appear at the said Court, to execute, pay, do, and perform their Offices, Rents, Suits, and Services, and you are to Summon twenty-four Substantial Men of the said Hundred and Manor, to appear at the said Court, to serve on the Jury, and Homage, and to enquire as well for the King as the Body of the said Hundred and Manor, and you are to appear at the said Court, and make a return of this Precept at your Peril.

Given under my Hand and Seal the 1st Day of October in the Year of our Lord, 1807.

[signed] Mr. Salisbury
Steward

[D.C.R.O. D.PIT/M72]

Haywards were responsible for the maintenance of hedges and enclosures, and received payment for animals on common land.

An Assizer was more or less equivalent to the present-day Weights and Measures Inspector, testing the weight or measure, quality and price of certain commodities, notably bread and beer.

William, for the latter part of his life, held The Bell Inn at Fiddleford. He died in 1749, aged 41, and was buried at Sturminster Newton on 5 December. Rose outlived him by 33 years and was buried, also at Sturminster Newton, on 30 November 1782, aged 82.

William and Rose Pitt had four children. Robert, the second son, was baptised at the Church of St. Mary, Sturminster Newton on 9 October 1734. At the age of 36 he married Mary Matcham, whom he met in Bath, at that time the centre of fashionable living. This perhaps substantiates Robert's reputation as someone who liked the good things of life.

The marriage, by licence, of *"Robert Pitt of the Parish of Bellchalwell Batchelor . . . . and Mary Matcham of this parish Spinster . . . "* took place at Child Okeford on 27 December 1770. The ceremony was conducted by the Curate, Richard H. Rogers: the witnesses were John Matcham and William Loveless.

Their children were:

George Matcham	baptised	29 June	1772	at	Stur. Newton		
Susanna	"	1 Apr,	1774	"	"	"	
Lucy	"	5 Aug.	1776	"	Child Okeford	buried 1776	
Lucy	"	9 Nov.	1777	"	"	"	
Thomas) "sons &	"	30 Jan.	1779	"	"	"	buried 1779
William) twins"	"	30 Jan.	1779	"	"	"	
Thomas	"	2 May	1781	"	Stur. Newton		
Jemima	"	10 June	1783	"	"	"	
Hester	"	9 July	1786	"	"	"	(father —

"Robert Pitt of Belchalvill")

The reason for Robert's *"distressed circumstances"* are not known, but his commitments in respect of various properties must have involved him in considerable expense.

17

In 1766, then 32 years of age and still a bachelor, he acquired the lease of a cottage in Fiddleford known as The Trout Ale-house. [D.C.R.O. D.PIT/T.341]

On 22 September 1779 he signed an indenture (as a shopkeeper) for premises in Child Okeford in the sum of £300. [D.C.R.O. D.PIT/T.603]

On the same day he signed the lease for Fiddleford Mill. [D.C.R.O. D.PIT/T.620]

On 18 November 1779 he was granted a loan (mortgage) by John Harrison (of which £129.14.0 plus interest had to be repaid when Robert finally admitted financial failure). [D.C.R.O. D.PIT/T.620]

A little less than a month later he signed another indenture for leasehold property in Newton, viz. *"all that messuage or tenement in Newton within the Manor of Sturminster Newton Castle with a garden and Orchard thereunto adjoining containing by estimation One Acre and One Fardel of Land of the Antient Tenure . . . . . . containing by estimation Eight Acres and two perches, be it more or less together with common of Pasture for three Rother Beasts in and upon a Certain Common there called by the name of Ralph Down, all of which premises were late in the possession of Margaret Matcham and now of William Belbin or his undertenant."* George Pitt, *"(about seven years old)"*, son of Robert Pitt was included. The fine for this was £42.0.0 and the rent £0.6.9 twice yearly. [D.C.R.O. D.PIT/T574]

This presumably was the *"tenement"* referred to in the Sturminster Newton Court Book [D.C.R.O. D.PIT/M.71] when, on 18 October 1779 it was *"Agreed with Robt. Pitt to grant one life, after his Uncle and himself, in the old man's tenement, worth £14 p. Ann. Fine £42."* On 18 October 1784 another entry reads *"They present that William Belbin died since the last Court and that Robt. Pitt is the Lords next Tenant."*

This property was left in the will (drawn up on 20 May 1763 and proved in 1766) of his aunt, Margaret Matcham. It was, of course, the most important item in the will, but the document makes interesting reading, bequeathing small personal items (such

18

as "*my best yellow quilted petty Coat*" *and* "*a Brass Pott*"), which today would not be considered worth mentioning.

"In the name of God Amen. I Margaret Matchem of Sturminster Newton in the County of Dorset Widow, considering the uncertainty of this mortal Life and being of sound Mind and memory, blessed be Almighty God for the same, do make and ordain this my last Will and Testament in manner and Form following. First I give unto my Brother William Belbin and my Sister Rose Pitt all that my Leasehold Estate lying in Sturminster Newton aforesaid known by the name of Yeatmans even and equally between them, for and during the Life of my said Brother William Belbin; and after his Decease I give my said Leasehold Estate unto my two Nephews Robert Pitt and William Pitt/ both Sons of my Sister Rose Pitt/ even and equally between them. I give unto my Brother Benjamin Belbin the Sum of five Pounds. I give unto my Brother Joseph Belbin the Sum of five Pounds. I give unto my Sister Betty Adams/ for her own private use/ the Sum of ten Pounds and if She survives her Husband I will and desire she might of quiet and peaceable possession of that dwelling now in Possession of James Short for and during her natural Life without paying of any Rent or Taxes whatsoever. I give unto my Sister Susan Stickland the Sum of five Pounds one Month after my Decease, and the Sum of five Pounds twelve Months after my Decease. I further give into my Sister Betty Adams my Camblett Goun, black quilted Petty Coat and my best Hatt. I give unto Betty Belbin, daughter of my Brother Robert Belbin the sum of five Pounds and my best Goun, my best yellow quilted petty Coat, my largest Kettle, a Brass Pott, one Barrel a Tubb & Trendle, one Diaper Table-Cloth, two Pewter Dishes, three Plates, one Box, one little Chest, one pair of Sheets, one pair of Pillowbier & one little Table Board. I give unto Susannah Rose, daughter of Christopher Rose, one Pewter Dish and two Plates. I give unto Mary Matchem and Hister Matchem/ my Husbands Brothers Daughters/ my ?nance equally between them. All which said Legacies I will and desire might be paid and fulfilled one Month after my Decease. And if any of the above mention'd Persons shall die/ to whom Legacies are given/ before me I will and desire that the said legacies shall belong to my Executor and Executrix hereinaftermention'd.

And lastly as to all the rest residue and remainder of my Personal Estates, goods and Chattles of what nature or kind soever, I give unto my Brother William Belbin and my Sister Rose Pitt even and equally between them and do hereby make them joynt Executor and Executrix of this my last Will and Testament hereby revoking all former Will or Wills by me made. In Witness whereof I have hereunto set my Hand and Seal this twentieth Day of May in the year of our Lord Christ One thousand seven hundred and sixtythree"

It seems that financial problems were not the only worries with which the Pitt family had to deal. An entry, 16 October 1780 in the Sturminster Newton Court records reads *"a grt deal of complaint from Pits wife, of bad behaviour of the old Tapper wom [woman] in Fidford house, resolved not to interfere therein any farther — Let par offrs remove her, if she is a real nuisance or likely to be chgble. A clamor also at Pew in y [the] Isles"* [D.C.R.O. D.PIT/M71] John Tapper had proposed William Pitt, Robert's father, for Colber Tythingman in 1737. Perhaps Robert and Mary had inherited from William Pitt the responsibility of housing *"the old Tapper woman"*, presumably of the same family as John Tapper.

"Robert Pitt of Bellchalvil" was buried at Sturminster Newton on

6 April 1787. His death, in his 53rd year, left his family in a desperate situation financially.

The Sturminster Newton Court Book records:

"Belchalwell:
Robert Pitt late Belbin 10/- [deleted]
2 years occupied by the widow of the late Robert Pitt in hand and held Rent Free by Lord Rivers bounty."

Barbara Lamble says "Robert was not regarded very highly among his early Australian descendants; but was he the feckless spendthrift they believed? Did a certain amount of bitterness at their situation come with them? That period in history was the beginning of great change in the lives of small country landholders. When one compares the signature on the 1785 document with previous examples, it is difficult to avoid having concern for him because, if he were not a sick man, it was perhaps the sign of a final admission of failure. He was a shopkeeper in Child Okeford and must have been unsuccessful. He had inherited a mill building obviously not maintained by his ageing uncle. Perhaps his wife, a determined woman by all accounts, had urged him beyond his capacity. I hope we shall discover the true story."

MARY PITT (nee MATCHAM)

George Matcham Pitt [1813-1896], grandson of Mary Pitt, wrote that she *"came originally from Ireland. Her father died, and her Mother married again, and she and her husband went to America. Mary Matcham crossed over to England and she lived with two maiden Aunts till death carried them away at 81 and 83 . . . . . Her Aunts left her some three different estates, not large ones . . . . . My grandfather* [Robert Pitt] *died young, and he left his widow not in good circumstances. She was of an high cast of character, and she sold what she had and finished her life here* [in Australia]*."*

It is virtually certain that Mary was the daughter of Thomas, the eldest son of Thomas Matcham and his wife Mary (nee Ford), who were married at Shillingstone. The Parish Register records "*30 June 1701 . . . . Thomas Macham and Mary Ford both of the parish of Child Okeford were married after Banns thrice published here, according to Mr. Crabbs certificate.*"

An entry in Burke's 'Gentry' of 1906 shows "*Mary daughter of Robert Pitt of Belchalwell married Thomas Matcham.*" Burke is not always reliable, and it seems obvious that the entry should read: "Mary daughter of Thomas Matcham married Robert Pitt of Belchalwell."

Mrs. Lamble writes . . . . . "The history of the sons of Thomas and Mary (FORD) MATCHAM is obscure after mention of them in their Uncle John MATCHAM's will written in 1734, other than Simon, who is well known. He joined the East India Company and became Superintendent of the Marine and senior member of the Council of Bombay. He was born on 7 April 1711, married Elizabeth, daughter of Hugh BIDWELL of Devon, a senior member of the Company in Bombay. He died on 22 January 1776 leaving one surviving son, George.

George was employed also by the East India Company. He was born on 30 November 1754 and married Catherine, younger daughter of the Rev. Edmund Nelson. He died on 3 February 1833."

George Matcham was first cousin to Mary Pitt (nee Matcham) and it was to him that she, a widow in straitened circumstances, eventually turned for help. He advised her to emigrate to Australia, and it was he who, through the Commissioner of the Navy, George Gambier, made the arrangements for her to travel to New South Wales.

George Matcham's wife, Catherine, was the younger sister of Lord Nelson, and George was guardian of Horatia, daughter of the Admiral and Emma Hamilton. It was his brother-in-law, Lord Nelson, who sponsored Mary Pitt and her family. George also sent a son of his own to N.S.W., and there is an area north of Sydney called Matcham.

Again quoting Mrs. Lamble — "I am not sure when Mary's position became intolerable, whether it was the deaths of her two older sons — "killed in America", pressure from her overlord or the future of her family, having two daughters of marriageable age with no dowries and two more on the way there, but the evidence is that she was a proud, independent woman who was not afraid to say or do what she thought right and would not live happily as she was then placed . . . She had been a widow for fourteen years before migration and fourteen years more here, and I feel that the Matcham influence was uppermost. This could apply to her mother-in-law, Rose PITT nee BELBIN, who was a widow from 1749-1782 with no obvious Pitt influence, just Belbins all around her."

The family settled in Australia in 1801. George Matcham Pitt, a grandson of Robert and Mary, was born in 1813. He was the great-grandfather of Barbara Lamble and she says that he "was born on the farm on the Hawkesbury River, a grant in 1802 to his father Thomas, who was probably born in May Cottage, Fiddleford in 1781.

George Matcham Pitt was a well-known identity in early N.S.W. and as a young man walked stock to the north-west of the state, bred from them and then walked those for sale back to Sydney — some hundreds of miles.

He founded a 'wool firm' in Sydney and was joined by his son, my grandfather Robert Matcham Pitt, who made it into the highly esteemed company it became. 'Wool Firms' were the centre of the rural industry here at that time; actually they were 'Stock and Station Agents'. Unfortunately there were no interested grandsons to keep it going and it was absorbed by a rival.

Although George Matcham Pitt moved to Sydney, he continued to work or lease the Richmond farms. He lived at first in Fairlight, a house which gave its name to a suburb of today. He was described at that time as "a portly old man who used to wear a straw boater and sat on the deck of the Manly steamers, full of fun and cracking jokes with the other passengers. The Pitts were members of the Anglican Church". ['Manly 1788-1968' by Charles Swancott]

23

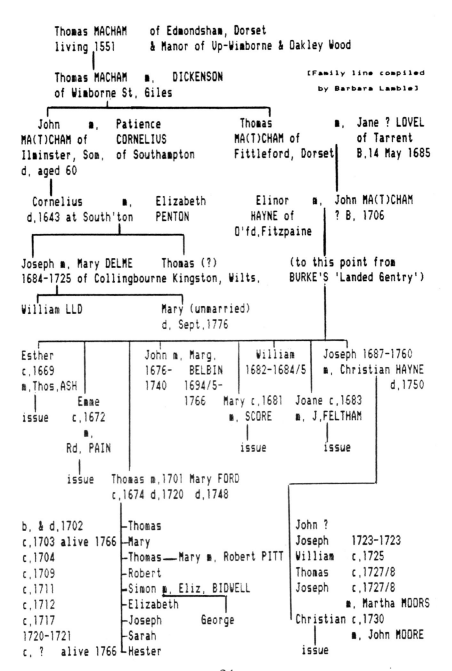

Thomas MACHAM   of Edmondsham, Dorset
living 1551   & Manor of Up-Wimborne & Oakley Wood

Thomas MACHAM   m. DICKENSON   [Family line compiled
of Wimborne St. Giles   by Barbara Lamble]

John   m. Patience   Thomas   m. Jane ? LOVEL
MA(T)CHAM of   CORNELIUS   MA(T)CHAM of   of Tarrent
Ilminster, Som, of Southampton Fittleford, Dorset B.14 May 1685
d. aged 60

Cornelius   m. Elizabeth   Elinor   m. John MA(T)CHAM
d.1643 at South'ton PENTON   HAYNE of   ? B. 1706
                                    O'fd.Fitzpaine

Joseph m, Mary DELME   Thomas (?)   (to this point from
1684-1725 of Collingbourne Kingston, Wilts,   BURKE'S 'Landed Gentry')

William LLD   Mary (unmarried)
                         d. Sept.1776

Esther   John m, Marg,   William   Joseph 1687-1760
c.1669   1676- BELBIN   1682-1684/5   m, Christian HAYNE
m,Thos,ASH   1740   1694/5-   d,1750
                           1766   Mary c,1681 Joane c,1683
        Emme   m, SCORE   m, J,FELTHAM
issue   c,1672   issue
        m,   issue
        Rd, PAIN

        issue   Thomas m,1701 Mary FORD
                c,1674 d,1720 d,1748

b, & d,1702   ⌐Thomas   John ?
c,1703 alive 1766 ⌐Mary   Joseph   1723-1723
c,1704   ⌐Thomas—Mary m, Robert PITT William c,1725
c,1709   ⌐Robert   Thomas   c,1727/8
c,1711   ⌐Simon m, Eliz, BIDWELL Joseph c,1727/8
c,1712   ⌐Elizabeth   m, Martha MOORS
c,1717   ⌐Joseph   George   Christian c,1730
1720-1721   ⌐Sarah   m, John MOORE
c, ?   alive 1766 ⌐Hester   issue

24

Mrs. Lamble continues: "Leaving Manly, G. M. Pitt moved to Holbrook, Carabella Street, North Sydney (now Kirribilli). He was an alderman of the St. Leonards Council and mayor for part of that time. A book written by I. Brodsky at the request of the North Sydney Council includes in the history of 1788-1962 the following story: *At Kirribilli G. M. Pitt took a special interest in what was called 'Pitts Spring' in Mount Street. A growing agitation for water ultimately resulted in water being piped across the harbour. This was the first water to be supplied for North Sydney from Botany. In 1885 a line of flexible pipes was laid down between Dawe's Point and Milson's Point permitting two million gallons to be pumped across daily. At a signal from Mr. Moriarty, Engineer in Chief, the water was turned on at Dawes Point, states the record. After a lapse of several minutes brownish water appeared and it tasted of salt, but presently "Quite fresh now, Sir" was the signal for satisfaction. G. M. Pitt was there that joyful day but it was with champagne not water that he and others toasted the great occasion.*"

Pitt Street, Kirribilli was named after him.

George Matcham Pitt died 12 October 1896 at Kirribilli of, according to his death certificate, *"chronic Bright's disease"* which he was said to have had for eight years.

His death and burial was freely reported in the Press. The description from one is as follows:

"As the procession moved through the streets of the sleepy old town [Richmond] every place of business was closed and not a soul was visible, apart from the long procession. As a hot wind swept across the flats, and the church bell tolled its deadly message, it seemed as though the whole place was in mourning for the man who had been born beside the river long ago. As the procession filed into the churchyard it passed the flower-covered grave of the brave young fellow who was drowned in the Hawkesbury on the Saturday before, a young man of 17. Here was this old man, G. M. Pitt, who had made his mark on the community after a long life of nearly 83 years, and was now being borne to his last rest by faithful friends. He had made his record, lived his life, a big framed big-hearted man, belonging to the old school, and now he was finished.

GEORGE MATCHAM PITT
1813 - 1896

None should weep for him. He had fought a good fight, fulfilled his years honourably, and left sons enough to bear him to the grave, good sons, honourable men, and what better record could a man desire . . . .

The men who started Homebush yards, or, rather the auction sales of fat stock, were men like — William Fullagar, Thomas Sullivan, Wm. Tindale, Thos. Dawson and G. M. Pitt. They were a grand crowd, and they worked for all they got. In 1874 G. M. Pitt took his son R. M. Pitt into the stock and station business under the title of G. M. Pitt and Son, then, as the business expanded, Mr. H. S. Badgery was invited to join and, as one of the best auctioneers in the country, he joined the firm in 1879, which became known as Messrs. Pitt, Son and Badgery.

After that, in 1888, it was made into a limited liability company, and of its fame and character there is no need to speak. The old gentleman remained as chairman till the day of his death.

Mr. G. M. Pitt, the founder of the firm, was a large-hearted generous man who bound us to the past in a remarkable manner. Though born in New South Wales he yet seemed to stand very close to the Matchams and in a very special sense he bound us to the old land. In New South Wales, too, he was the link between the fat stock men of today and the ante-salesyards days of an almost forgotten time. He was a grand old landmark, and in losing him, we lose one of the noblest of the fast-perishing pioneer race . . . . .

The funeral of G. M. Pitt was a great and notable event in our history, and we can well say that, taking him for all in all 'we ne'er shall look upon his like again'. His epitaph might well be written: 'Noble he was. Condemning all things mean. His truth unquestioned and his soul serene'."

Barbara Lamble concludes: "G. M. Pitt's participation in Pitt, Son and Badgery was minimal towards the end of his life, his son, R. M. Pitt, managing the Firm. A grand-daughter described him as a sick old man, but never was his position down-graded while he lived. He was a generous, philanthropic man, who gave freely without fanfare.

During the last years of his life there was instability in the business and banking world of New South Wales. Administration of his affairs was necessarily influenced by the financial situation. This period belongs to the history of the life of his son, R. M. Pitt or 'Old Bob' as everyone knew him. Holbrook, the home in Kirribilli, became the property of his son Robert and his family until it was sold in 1916."

ROBERT MATCHAM PITT
1849-1935

28

JOB ROSE

Job Rose was probably the most well-known miller in North Dorset — famous for his immense size, which inspired William Barnes to immortalise him in his poem John Bloom in Lon'on. He reputedly weighed about 440 lbs., i.e. in the region of 200 kgs. — and in the latter years of his life, unable to climb the stairs, he slept in the strong, roomy oak chair which had been made especially for him.

Oak chair made for Job Rose

29

James Herridge and his wife Mary (Job's daughter) went on a visit to the Holyland, and the olive-wood stick which is leaning against the chair in the picture was a gift which they brought back for Tom Rose, Mary's brother.

Job's loving cup, now in the possession of his great grandson, bears the traditional farmers' verse:

Let the Wealthy & Great
Roll in Splendor & State
I envy them not I declare it
I eat my own Lamb
My Chickens and Ham
I shear my own Fleece & I wear it
I have Lawns, I have Bow'rs
I have Fruits, I have Flow'rs
The Lark is my morning alarmer
So jolly Boys now
Here's God Speed the Plough
Long Life and success to the Farmer

Thomas Hardy mentioned these large two-handled drinking vessels in Far From The Madding Crowd, referring to the one he described as a God-forgive-me. In Chapter 8 the maltster says " 'Come, shepherd, and drink . . . . . Take up the God-forgive-me, Jacob. See if 'tis warm, Jacob.' Jacob stooped to the God-forgive-me, which was a two-handled tall mug . . . . . It may be observed that such a class of mug is called a God-forgive-me in Weatherbury and its vicinity for uncertain reasons: probably because its size makes any given toper feel ashamed of himself when he sees its bottom in drinking it empty." [A toper is an excessive or habitual drinker]

Job came from an old Sturminster Newton family, his great-grandparents being Thomas Rose and Rebecca, nee Topp, who married at Sturminster Newton 8 February 1745.

Job's grandparents were Robert Rose (second son of Thomas and Rebecca) and Sarah Lambert, whose marriage took place at Sturminster Newton in June 1770. Robert and Sarah had a large family — at least nine children — James, baptised in 1788, being one of the younger ones.

James, a labourer, married Charlotte Fudge at Sturminster Newton in August 1811, and Job, their firstborn, arrived 15 July 1812. At least eight more children followed.

Job's marriage to Hannah Chaffey was in April 1838, and they too brought up a large family of eight children, the first two being born whilst they were living in one of a row of cottages (now demolished) opposite Sturminster Bridge.

Job Rose, although the tenant of Fiddleford Mill from 1855 until his son Samuel took over in 1871, never lived at Fiddleford. According to Mr. Jim Oliver, a great-grandson, Job went to Woodbridge Mill at Bedchester (near Fontmell Magna) in 1844. Soon after this, the house was damaged by fire, most of it being burnt down. Apart from the kitchen, the trap house and the part at the back near the mill race, the present Woodbridge Mill dates from the mid-19th century.

Job was an active Wesleyan Methodist, and it is obvious from a letter he wrote to a Mrs. Spencer that he was a devout Christian.

1.

Woodridge Hill
Saturday

Mrs Spencer
Dear Madame
I received your likeness
I was very pleased with
it, it brought to my
mind by gone days when
you used to run about
from place to place visit
-ing the sick Chamber
administering to there wants
by sending me of with
the basket & bottle to
comfort them ——

2.

Dear Madame,
I shall never forget
that Motherly Kindness
you showed me when
a youth at your House
especially in Keeping me
in Sunday night & not
letting me out with the
rabble I only wish the same
was done now it would
prevent the youth from
running into a great deal
of mischief;

3.

but now dear Madame
it hath pleased the Lord
to lay in afflicting hand
on me & if my affliction
should terminate in death
I trust I shall be ready,
prepared to meet Christ
at is coming & that my
lamp will be trimd &
light burning ready to
go in to the marriage
supper of Lamb & if
I should never see your
dear familiar face
no more on earth

4.

I trust I shall meet
you in Heaven where
we shall sing Gods
praises together through
an eternal day

my love to Mrs Hames
& likewise to the rest
part of your household
& believe me to be
faithfully yours in
Christ
Jeff Rose

excuse bad writing

32

Woodbridge Mill
Saturday

Mrs. Spencer

Dear Madame

I receivd your likeness. I was very pleased with it, it brought to my mind bygone days when you used to run about from place to place visiting the sick Chamber administering to there wants by sending me of with the basket & bottle to comfort them.

Dear Madame, I shall never forget that Motherly Kindness you showed me when a youth at your House especially in keeping me in Sunday night & not letting me out with the rebels I only wish the same was done now it would prevent the youth from running into a great deal of mischief.   but now Dear Madame it hath pleased the Lord to lay is afflicting hand on me & if my afflictions should terminate in Death I trust I shall be ready prepared to meet Christ at is coming & that my lamp will be primed & light burning ready to go in to the marriage supper of Lamb & if I should never see your dear familiar face no more on earth I trust I shall meet you in Heaven where we shall sing God's praises together through our eternal day.

My love to Mrs. Kaines [?] & likewise to the rest part of your household & believe me to be faithfully yours in Christ

[signed]   *Job Rose*

excuse bad writing

Unfortunately the letter is undated, but it seems likely that it was written towards the end of his life.

Job Rose died 9 February 1871 and was buried beside the old Chapel at Hartgrove. The grave, surrounded by black iron railings, was photographed by Jim Oliver some years ago. All visible traces of it have now disappeared, both the old and new disused Chapels (which stand side by side) having been converted to private houses with gardens.

Job's Will, signed 29 January 1870 in the presence of George Genge and James Burbidge of Shaftesbury, was proved at Blandford 12 June 1871.

His estate was left in trust for his wife Hannah during her lifetime, the trustees being the executors of the will — Charles Godwin, Shroton, brewer, and Richard Bartlett Warren of Child Okeford, farmer. His wife and son Tom were to carry on *"the several trades or businesses in which I shall be engaged at the time of my decease"*, and should they be sold at any time, Tom was to be given the option of purchasing the trades/businesses. Provision was made for any unmarried daughters under the age of twenty-one, and sums of money were bequeathed *"to my daughter Mary Herridge"* and to some of his other children.

[D.C.R.O. mic/R/396/1871/178]

Job's sons stayed within a few miles of their birthplace, all four following his occupation at local mills. Three — Samuel, James and Charles remained millers until their deaths.

The following generations, however, went farther afield, and descendants of Job's daughters, Sarah and Kate, are living in Germany and New Zealand.

JOB ROSE'S SONS

TOM ROSE

At the time of Job's death, his eldest sons were already managing mills of their own — Samuel at Fiddleford and James at Sturminster Newton [see Where Elm Trees Grew] — so it was natural that the remaining two sons — Tom (26) and Charles (24) should carry on at Woodbridge Mill. Hannah, Job's widow, was described in the 1871 Census Returns as 'miller', but this was no doubt because she was head of the household and held the lease.

Hannah Rose (nee Chaffey) 1815-1895
wife of Job Rose

35

1876. Monday March 27th.

Hannah Robbins Bag Flour	1	10 0
Robt Hunt 1/2 Do	1	0 0
Fred Hawkins 1/2 Bag Do	1	0 0
Amos Barber 3 Ackts Barley	2	11 0
John Hazle 1/2 Cwt Bran		1 6
Wm ——— 1/2 Cwt Sharps		2 0
Very busy Putt about our flour from together		

Tuesday 28th.

Fred Robins 6 Bags Flour	10	10 0
Mr Tapper 1 Sack Barley	1	7 0
Do 1 Bag Old Wheat		3 0
2 Bags Putt load of sand from Brampton		

Wednesday 29th.

Mr Burge 10 Bags Flour	17	0 0
Do 2 Ackts Maize	1	15 0
Do 5 Ackts Barley	5	17 6
Do 4 Cwt Sharps	1	8 0
Do 4 Cwt Bran	1	0 0
Robt Fisher 2 Bags Flour	3	12 0
John Hazle 2 Cwt Sharps		16 0
Do Cwt Bran		6 0

Thursday 30th.

Mr Smith 10 Bags Flour	17	0 0
Mr Wright Cwt Bran		6 0
Mr Taylor 1/2 Sk Barley		9 0
Mr J Miles 2 Cwt Sharps		16 0
Do Sack Barley		18 0
Mr J Miles 2 Cwt Sharps		16 0
Received from Melbourge found up		
One Horse hard load of sand from Brampton		

1876. Friday March 31st.

Mr G Burge 5 Acts Barly	4	0 0
Do 2 Acts Maize	1	15 0
Mr Baines 5 Acts Barley	4	0 0
Do 4 Cwt Sharps	1	8 0
Do 4 Cwt Bran	1	0 0
Do 2 Acts Maize	1	———
Mr Dyke 2 Acts Barley	1	16 0
Do 4 Cwt Sharps	1	8 0
Henry Flohat Cwt Do		8 0
Cent Amy Gill cart have for breakfast		

Saturday April 1st.

Henry Hawkins Bag Flour	1	16 0
S Hunt Bag Do	1	16 0
Hannah Robbins Do	1	16 0
Wm Throne 1/2 Bag Do	1	0 0
Mr G Baines 10 Bags Do	17	0 0
Mr Mr Day Cwt Bran w wheat		
Mr Wright 1/2 Sk Wheat		2 0
John Hazle Cwt Sharps		8 0
Do Cwt Bran		6 0
Mr Giles Sack Barley		18 0
Mr H Day Sack Do		18 0
Hannah Robbins Paid	3	0 0
Bag Putt load Sand to Chappel		

Monday 3rd.

Mr Whitworth 4 Bags Flour	7	0 0
Do Cwt Sharps		7 0
Do Cwt Bran		5 0
Mr Tanker Peck Meal		2 0
Mr John Day Cwt Sharps		8 0
(New Here)		

There is an Account Book for Woodbridge — a photograph of a week's entries from the Ledger for March 1876 is shown on the previous page. The sales of wheat, barley etc. were recorded, and presumably as payment was made the entries were crossed through. One particularly interesting item is a load of lime for the new *"Chappel"* at Hartgrove. Jim Oliver says that the handwriting is that of his grandfather, Tom Rose.

By the time the 1881 Census was recorded, Charles was working Woodbridge Mill on his own, Tom having left, with his mother Hannah, to become a farmer at Bedchester.

Bedchester Farm House c. 1904
Used as a dairyman's residence and cheese room when replaced by house across the road

Bedchester Cross, showing Shop/Post Office and Chapel c. 1904

On 14 February 1884, at Manston Church, Tom married Ann Emily Hunt of Swainscombe Farm, Hartgrove. John Tapper was best man. The gift of a clock from the Hartgrove Sunday School marked the occasion. The inscription reads:

Presented to
Tom Rose
By the Friends Teachers and
Scholars of the Hartgrove
Sunday School
On the Occasion of His
Marriage
14th February 1884

Tom Rose kept a diary which gives an interesting insight into the life of a typical farmer in the last quarter of the 19th century.

A few excerpts from this journal, which faithfully records the day-to-day happenings at Bedchester Farm, are reproduced. It seems to have been a humdrum existence, the only relief being provided by the Chapel meetings.

1886

Jan. 1 "Settled with all the Men. David and Herbert with 3 Horses all day pulling down Chalk off Hill into yard — Alfred all day cracking stones there — "

The month of January was spent pulling down chalk, mending cribs and working with the dung cart. Ploughing and chain harrowing were the main jobs in February.

Feb. 15 "We all Thrashed 30 Sks. Wheat and 12 Sks. Beans"

Feb. 19 "David at home all day. Alfred & Herbert with the 4 horses all day pulling stone from Compton into yard. Then Herbert pulled back Mr. Drew of [?] Melbury"

March 20 "Little Frank Hill came on to work with Alfred stone picking"

March 29 "I went to Gillingham and bot [sic] Cow & Calf 9-17-6 [£9.87p]"

April 7 "The little boy drove in with the wet"

In April "I and the boy and Elizabeth couch picking"

April 23 (Good Friday) "Settled with all the men. All the men at home working for themselves. We went to Chapel and had a good Tea Meeting. Our Sallie and Children came down."

Monday, April 26 (Bank Holiday) "David, Herbert & Alfred sowed the Barley in 8 Acres — The boy digging docks in the wheat. We gave the Children their Tea at Chapel"

Monday, June 7 "Wife Confined today at 4 o'clock"

June 26 "Garland came over and rung the Bull"

Friday, July 2 "Our Baby christened today"

Friday, July 16 "We all went to Shroton and Polled"

Sept. 10 (Friday) "Settled with all the men and boy for day work and harvesting, and paid them 2/6 [12½p] each for a dinner"

39

Sept. 13 "Alfred and the boy gone to Wood Nutting"

Sept. 14 "We all carried our Clover"

Sept. 15 "We all carried our Barley"

Alfred nutting five or six days

Oct. 25 "David, Herbert and Alfred began Wheat sowing in Briers. The boy and I taking up Couch in Markland"

Thursday, Nov. 11 "All the Brethren here to our Missionary Meeting"

Dec. 8 "John Garrett had 10 Sks. Oats 8/- [40p]

Dec. 25 "All the Men at home. I went up to Chapel and heard Fred Sankey preach. John Tapper Wife and Children came over and spent the day with us. A splendid day — "

Dec. 31 "My birthday today 42 years"

The Chapel obviously played a big part in the life of the Rose family. Tom was superintendent, and when he died, his sister Kate's husband, John Tapper, took over.

Tom and Ann had three daughters — Annie, Mary Kate (mother of Jim Oliver) and Carrie. The first two girls were named after Tom's sisters.

Tom died 7 September 1900 and was buried at Fontmell Magna. He had conscientiously continued his journal, though from April 1900 onwards his writing became increasingly shaky, and some entries were made by Tom's daughter Mary, although she was only thirteen years old.

On the day of Tom's death, Mary recorded in pencil *"Settled with all the men. Toomer ploughing in Briers. Roe in garden digging potatoes. John, Roe and . . . ? . . . . . fencing in Read's Ground, and doing odd things."* Written vertically, in ink, by Mary's mother Ann Emily across this entry (obliterating the name of the third man engaged in fencing) is a simple sentence: *"Darling father died at 10.10 in the eve."*

40

On 12 September, a note in the journal reads *"All the men doing odd things in the morning and went to poor father's funeral in the afternoon."*

Tom's widow, Ann Emily, left Bedchester Farm in 1919, retiring to Hambledon Cottage, Child Okeford. She died in January 1929, when she was 80 years old, and was buried beside her husband.

Ann Emily Rose (nee Hunt), daughter of Harry and Harriet Hunt
of Swainscombe, Hartgrove
May 1848 - January 1929
(photo 1919)

Annie Rose
(photo — late 1930's)

Annie, eldest daughter of Tom and Ann Emily, never married. She was born in December 1884 and died in 1949. She is buried at Child Okeford.

Mary Kate, the second daughter, was born at Bedchester Farm 6 June 1886. In November 1912, at Fontmell Magna Church, she married George F. Oliver, a farmer. They lived at Andrews Farm, Bedchester until 1919, when they moved to Fontmell Parva. In 1933, after six years at Chesham in Buckinghamshire, they settled at Send in Surrey, where they spent the rest of their lives — Mary died in June 1962. There were two sons of the marriage — Jim, who still lives in the family home in Surrey, and the younger Fred who died in 1983.

George Frederick Oliver and his son Jim at Fontmell Parva

Mary Kate Oliver (nee Rose) and son Jim
(photo 1938)

43

Carrie, Tom Rose's youngest daughter, became the wife of Stanley H. Edwards when he came back home to Fontmell Magna after serving in the First World War. They had two sons — Philip George and Mark.

Dorset Waggon used at Bedchester Farm, and reputedly made for Job Rose about 1840 by Beale, wheelwright and blacksmith at Sturminster Bridge. The waggon was used by the Olivers at Send Court Farm until the end of the 1939-45 war.

(l. to r.) Henry Beale, A. Beale, James Beale, J. Watts
Wheelwrights and Blacksmiths, The Bridge, Sturminster Newton

The Beale workshop (actually two buildings) was opposite the Bull Inn, between the Bridge and Rose's Garage on the river side of what is now the A.357. Ron Beale, born in Sturminster Newton, but who now lives at Portesham in West Dorset, confirmed that the photograph was probably taken around the turn of the century, i.e. 1900 or soon after, and shows his great-grandfather (always known to Ron's mother as 'Grandfather Beale') second from the left. James (Ron's grandfather) and Henry were both blacksmiths, and another son, Sidney, was a wheelwright and waggon maker.

Sidney built an iron rowing boat, about twelve feet long, which he painted green. It was moored in the river beside the workshops and well-known in the area, was always referred to as 'Uncle Sid's green boat'. It was rather odd that it was he, the wheelwright, and not his blacksmith brothers, who built an iron boat!

There was another brother, George, who lived in Okeford Fitzpaine.

After working with Sidney and their father for some years, James and Henry eventually bought a plot in Bath Road, next to the British Legion premises, and started their own blacksmith's business, c. 1912.

* * * * * * * * * *

CHARLES ROSE

Little is known about Charles Rose, Job's youngest son. In 1881 Charles was the miller at Woodbridge Mill [according to the 1881 Census Returns]. He lived there with his wife Fanny. But Fanny died within the next three years, as the Fontmell Magna Register records the marriage, 28 February 1884, of Charles Rose, widower, aged 34, miller (son of Job Rose deceased) and Ellen Woolridge, spinster, aged 33 (daughter of Mark Woolridge deceased). (The entry in the Register shows Ellen's and her father's surname as *Woolridge*, but her signature is plainly *Wooldridge*.)

On 19 July 1884 Charles signed his Will in the presence of two witnesses, Emma Jane Stowell and Frederick Willmot, groom, both of St. James, Shaftesbury. The contents were straightforward — *"all my estate both real and personal unto my Wife Ellen Rose and I appoint her my said Wife and my friend Herbert Stowell of St. James Shaftesbury High Bailiff of the Shaftesbury County Court Executrix and Executor of this my last Will and Testament."*

On 29 September 1884 Probate of this Will was granted at Blandford to Ellen Rose, Charles's widow. [D.C.R.O. MIC/R/460/1884/209] So he, like his brother James (who was 32), died at an early age. He was 37.

There had been a Miller Rose at Woodbridge Mill for forty years, but Charles's death brought a change. The 1891 Census Returns show that the new miller was not a Dorset man, though strangely enough he was another Job!

46

The family was recorded as:

Woodbridge					Place of Birth	
Job	Moyle	52		miller	Hants.	Shirley
Sarah	Moyle	55	wife		Hants.	Sopley
Emily	Moyle	25	daughter		Hants.	Sopley
Sidney	May	25	nephew	Miller's asst.	Wilts.	Milston

Tom Haskell 1851 - 1872

Gourd's Farm, East Compton

JOB ROSE'S DAUGHTERS

MARY

Mary, second child and eldest daughter of Job and Hannah Rose, was born c. 1841. She was living at home with her parents in 1861, but when the Census was recorded in 1871 she was not included with other members of her family at Woodbridge Mill. Of course she could have been away temporarily, but it seems more probable that by that time she had married and was living in Gillingham (Dorset) with her husband, James Herridge.

Until her marriage Mary had been organist at Hartgrove Wesleyan Chapel, a duty which was then taken on by her sister Kate. James Herridge was also an active Wesleyan, and allegedly gave a considerable financial contribution towards the building of the Chapel in Gillingham. No more is known about Mary and her family.

* * * * * * * * * *

ANNIE

Little information is available about Annie, apart from the fact that she married a Mr. Rebbeck, whose family were farmers at Twyford.

* * * * * * * * * *

SARAH

Known to the family as Sally, she was born at Woodbridge Mill c. 1852, and in 1870 married Tom Haskell, born 29 November 1851. Tom died at the age of 20, and was buried at Fontmell Magna in April 1872. Sarah later married John King.

49

Her descendants in New Zealand have supplied the following information, which is reproduced in the writer's own words:

"Some Rose Descendants in the Antipodes

These notes on the descendants (who emigrated to New Zealand) of 'Girt' Job Rose of Woodbridge Mill have been compiled from the recollections of some of the descendants of Job's daughters Sarah and Kate, and written in collaboration by some of Sarah's descendants — i.e. Olive Matheson (eldest daughter of Sarah's son, Vic Haskell), with her daughter and son, Isobel Bretherton and Alister Matheson — in New Zealand.

Sarah Rose

In 1870 Sarah Rose married a farmer named Tom Haskell. He was a son of John Haskell (for forty years Churchwarden of the parish of Fontmell Magna) and Mary Ann Stay. The Haskell family had held the lease of Moore's Farm in Fontmell Magna since the late sixteenth century and had resided in the parish for at least a century before that.

Tom and Sarah had two children, John Victor and Mary Hannah Thomasine (known to all as Sis). There is some evidence that they farmed first at Bedchester and then at Compton Abbas. At the latter place they probably had Gourd's Farm, which was later run by Tom's brother, John G. Haskell.

According to family tradition, Tom bred hunting horses, besides other farming activities. Tom died as the result of a hunting accident in April 1872. His daughter was born some weeks later.

In 1874 Sarah Haskell married John King and went to live at Wickwood Farm, near Tisbury, Wiltshire. As far as is known the children of this marriage were (not necessarily in order of seniority): Harry, who married but had no children; Tom, who died unmarried in New Zealand; Amy, who married Stanley Hunt

50

[a Shaftesbury greengrocer] and had one daughter, Yvonne, who married George Lawrence; Kate, who married Mr. Stainer [in business in Shaftesbury as an undertaker and furniture retailer]; Gertrude, who married Mr. Genge and went to Canada; Elizabeth, who died young about the mid-1890's.

Amy King

Sarah King, formerly Haskell, daughter of Job and Hannah Rose
Photograph early 1900's

John King, second husband of Sarah (nee Rose)
photograph early 1900's

Vic Haskell

J. V. (Vic) Haskell
about 16 years old

Mary Hannah Thomasine (Sis) Haskell
1872 - 1956

children of Sarah (nee Rose) and Tom Haskell

When still very young both Vic and Sis Haskell were sent to boarding school. Vic is known to have attended Tisbury Academy and later Shaftesbury Grammar. When at school he had hoped for a career in the Navy. However, after leaving school in 1886 he found employment with Marshall and Snelgrove, a reputable tailor's and men's outfitter's in the West End of London. His cousin, Jim Tapper, recalled that he did very well with that firm and *"cut a great dash in top hat and morning coat"*. Nevertheless, his mother, Sarah King, expressed the view that the job was *"not good enough for Vic"*. Her daughter, Amy Hunt, remembered this when discussing those times with Vic's son, D'Arcy Haskell, when he visited England in 1972.

As Vic's subsequent career in New Zealand proved, his mother was correct in her opinion of his London job. It seems certain too that Vic himself wanted something better. At any rate, his cousin, Jim Tapper, said that as soon as he came into his inheritance he

53

left for New Zealand. Whether or not he had thought about New Zealand for any length of time beforehand, his actual departure for that country appears to have been precipitated by a slight disagreement with his uncle, George Haskell, who was a Cambridge graduate and a private tutor by occupation.

It seems that his uncle wanted him to go with him to the Holy Land to get water from the River Jordan to dedicate a chapel he had had built. This did not appeal to Vic and there is a suggestion that he feared his uncle hoped he would find a vocation in the Church, so he responded by saying *"I'm sorry, Uncle, but I've promised a friend to go to New Zealand."* He then had to make hurried arrangements to book his passage!

Opening of the railway line to Ethelton, Canterbury, New Zealand.
Photo 1906 — by Vic Haskell or Tom King

On the way to New Zealand, via South Africa, Vic stopped for a time in Western Australia, where gold had just been struck and the excitement was tremendous. He had never heard such noise as emanated from an hotel in Perth. As he had by this time decided to become a surveyor, he gained valuable experience of the elementary stages of this profession under John Forrest, afterwards going on to New Zealand, where he took up a cadetship with a private firm of surveyors.

In the late 1890's he returned to Western Australia, where he ran the levels for the Coolgardie water supply scheme, in which water was to be piped several hundred miles across the desert from Mundaring, near Perth, to the goldfields. He met his future wife in Western Australia.

After returning to New Zealand Vic was for a time with the Lands and Survey Department, and in 1901 he joined the Public Works Department as an authorised surveyor and civil engineer. He then worked in various parts of New Zealand, surveying routes for new railways and afterwards supervising their construction, including tunnels, bridges and viaducts, until his retirement in 1931.

Vic Haskell was an entertaining and witty raconteur with a fund of stories about his life in Dorset, Wiltshire, London, Australia and New Zealand. Of his grandfather, Job Rose, he recalled that there was a saying in Dorset that *"there was only room for Joe Rose and his cheque book in his dog cart"*. [Apparently Vic Haskell always referred to Job Rose as 'Joe']

When Vic was a little boy at boarding school he always of course returned to his stepfather's home at Wickwood Farm for the holidays (the school was within walking distance). That first night at home he always walked in his sleep to his mother's bedside and told her everything that had happened at school during the term. When he had finished she said *"Now go back to bed, Vic"*.

From about the age of five Vic followed the hounds hunting with the South Wilts. and the Blackmore Vale. He said that whenever he suffered a fall his pony nuzzled him till he got up.

A great reader all his life, Vic Haskell was at an early age familiar with the works of Dickens, Harrison Ainsworth and Hardy. He was deeply interested in the history of the Dorset-Wiltshire region, and, as a youth, enjoyed reading about past events on the sites where they had occurred.

When asked by his daughter, Olive, if he had ever seen crinoline dresses, he replied that he had seen them in wardrobes at home and that he had used the springs from them 'for his guns'! Presumably they were air guns.

When Vic was a youngster the country people really believed that ghostly funeral processions passed their houses at night and reckoned they heard them. Another curious tale he told concerned an empty room containing only a heap of sand. It was believed that the room was haunted by a ghost whose sin could only be absolved when he had made a rope of sand. Although Vic did not identify the building containing the haunted room, he said that he and his half-brother, Tom King, climbed a ladder to look in the window of the room and saw the heap of sand. A modern mind might suspect that both tales had their origin in old time smugglers' cover stories to frighten curious and talkative children from taking too keen an interest in the transport and storage of contraband.

There were many colourful and amusing incidents in Vic's life in Western Australia and New Zealand, too many to record here. One of the most extraordinary occurred in 1912, when, shortly after arriving in Kawakawa, one of his children's health caused such concern that he rang the hospital to ask for a doctor to call. Later, when he opened the door to the doctor, he stood back in astonishment and exclaimed "Good God! Eccles!". It was his old friend, Horace Dorset Eccles, whom he had not seen since schooldays. The doctor had come to New Zealand after service in the Boer War and marriage to a New Zealand nurse. It was a sad occasion for all the Haskell family when he left for England to enlist in the Army after the outbreak of World War I. He was later killed in action in France.

Vic and Ethel Haskell with four of their children, from left: D'Arcy (Doc), Blanche (Biddy), Amy, Olive — photographed by Tom King with Vic's camera at Ethelton, New Zealand in 1906

Vic Haskell himself did his best to enlist but was refused with the remark, "You've got six children".

About the time of the Armistice in November 1918 Vic Haskell and one of his clerks were among the few unaffected by the influenza pandemic, in which thousands died in New Zealand. However, large numbers of the railway construction workers, especially the Austrians, were stricken and Vic housed and nursed them all in a large railway shed, arranging bedding, medical treatment etc. with the help of his clerk. The men were so grateful for the way in which he had cared for them they called him 'Doctor' Haskell.

Vic mixed easily with all classes of society and was always popular with his workmen, both European and Maori. One of his cooks in his early years with the Public Works Department, who became a leading trade unionist and Labour member of Parliament and a life-long friend, was the central figure in an incident Vic often recalled. Once, when the inspecting engineer came to check a section of railway just completed under Vic's supervision the party was at dinner when the cook 'danced in' bearing a plate with a round plum pudding on it and proudly announced, "You wouldn't think this little b....r weighed eighteen pounds, but it does!", to which the inspecting engineer responded, "You wouldn't think you were going to get the sack tomorrow, but you are!"

Another of Vic's excellent workmen in the early years of the century became a very prominent trade unionist and an outstanding Minister of Public Works in the first Labour Government in New Zealand.

Whenever one section of railway was finished and Vic and his family were about to move to another district a 'smoke concert' or 'shevoo' was given. Vic's eldest daughter, Olive, attended some of these 'shevoos' as a youngster and remembers her father being carried shoulder high around the hall by his men as they sang 'For He's a Jolly Good Fellow'. When he was leaving one railway works in 1903 the men presented him with an illuminated address, in which they stated that they had "never had the pleasure

58

Some of Vic Haskell's railway survey party near Kaikoura, 1908-09
Far left — Mr. Genge, who later married Gertrude, youngest daughter of
Sarah (nee Rose) and John King
Second from right — Jim Tapper

of working under a more pleasant, just and considerate Engineer" and
were *"as one in regretting your departure from among us . . . "*

Vic Haskell loved music, as apparently did all his mother's
children. His daughter, Olive, recalls that he said 'the girls' could
go to a musical show and come home and play the music from
memory.

Vic had a fine baritone voice and frequently broke into the songs
of Gilbert and Sullivan about the house. He much enjoyed
musical evenings, either at home or at the houses of friends on
sheep stations in Canterbury Province. At home, accompaniment
on the piano was provided by his wife, Ethel, or daughter, Olive.
All the old favourites were sung: 'White Wings', 'Oft in the Stilly

J.O. Haskell. Esq.

Sir

We the Workmen on the Midland Railway Works, wish to make to you some acknowledgement of our appreciation of your worth. We have never had the pleasure of working under a more pleasant, just and considerate Engineer.

We are as one in regretting your departure from among us, but at the same time wish you every success in the new and advanced position you are taking up on the Waiharo - Christ Railway Works.

Wishing you and family long life, success and happiness.

We are.

for the Workmen
Yours very faithfully.

July 19 03

Midland Railway Works Springfield. Canterbury

H. B. Davis
W.H. Davis Junr.
A. Cameron
H. Bag___
W. Wakefield
Geo. Hutchison
Sinclair
H. Read
F. G. Maddison
Chas R. Gardner

60

Night', 'Juanita' etc., together with the songs of Stephen Foster and Gilbert and Sullivan.

As a very keen photographer, Vic always took his Thornton-Picard half-plate camera wherever he went in New Zealand and had dark rooms built at his different residences.

After his retirement in 1931, Vic and the younger members of his family lived in Auckland until 1934, when he went to manage the farm for the estate of his deceased half-brother, Tom King, at Toatoa. Vic died at Opotiki in 1945. He is remembered as one to whom everyone — children and adults alike — could go with their problems. He was in every way, as one lady put it, *"the perfect English gentleman"*.

Vic and Ethel Haskell's children at Te Puke, New Zealand, 1911/12
From left: D'Arcy (Doc), Blanche (Biddy), Olive holding Francesca (Bess), Amy, George

Vic Haskell in later life

Vic and Ethel Haskell had six children: Olive Constance, D'Arcy Ormonde (Doc), Challys Amy Berenice, Blanche Sarah (Biddy), George Thomas and Francesca Kate Elizabeth (Bess). D'Arcy became a distinguished civil engineer with the Public Works Department and George a marine engineer and later a farmer. Both carried out valuable work for the Allied cause in the South Pacific islands in World War II.

Vic Haskell's mother, Sarah King, died in 1908 and was buried at Cann Church, as was her husband, John, about two years later.

Vic's sister, Sis, never married and stayed at home to help her mother. Later she lived with her half-sister, Amy Hunt (nee King), and her husband Stanley, and helped them with their business. They lived in retirement in Bournemouth, where Sis died in 1956.

When D'Arcy (Doc) Haskell visited England in September/October 1972 Amy, then a widow, was living with her daughter, Yvonne, and her husband, George Lawrence. Amy was a

Christian Scientist and amazingly active at the age of 86. She thought nothing of walking eight miles to church!

Tom King

Tom King as a young man in England, early 1900's

Once Vic Haskell had settled in his career with the Public Works Department he encouraged other members of his family to migrate to New Zealand. His half-brother, Tom King, came out in 1905 and worked with a private surveyor, Mr. Dobson, on many interesting projects in the South Island. He later joined the Public Works Department. During World War I he served with the New Zealand Expeditionary Force in France, and on his return took up a farm at Toatoa.

Tom King before leaving New Zealand for France in World War I

In the 1920's he suddenly developed diabetes. He then broke off his engagement to be married, as he had no wish to be a burden to a wife. Thereafter his health was very poor and early in 1934, feeling very ill, he asked a neighbour to drive him to Vic Haskell's home in Auckland, a day's drive away, but died on the way there. Vic and all his family had been devoted to Tom and had often stayed with him at Toatoa. Vic immediately took over the management of the farm for his estate.

Tom King's homestead on his farm at Toatoa, N.Z., photographed in 1941 when his estate was managed by his half-brother Vic Haskell. The farm boundary runs across the valley to the right of buildings.

Like Vic, Tom often spoke of his early life in England. He said that as a youngster he was often at Stonehenge, and also that he played tennis at Fonthill Gifford Rectory. He told of a boy at his boarding school (presumably Tisbury Academy) who was so greedy he always grabbed the biggest of everything in the way of food and was only cured when he found a woolly turnip inside his large apple dumpling!

Two Englishmen, Stanley Hunt and Mr. Genge, who later married Tom King's sisters, Amy and Gertrude respectively, came out to New Zealand and worked for a time in Vic Haskell's survey party between about 1908 and 1912.

Jim Tapper

Vic Haskell's cousin, Jim Tapper, and his wife Susannah (nee Millard) arrived in New Zealand in 1906. They left England in April, and after landing went straight to Cheviot in Canterbury Province, in 1907 going on to the settlement of Domett, where the Haskells were then living.

As Jim told Vic's grand-daughter, Isobel Bretherton, in 1966, he and Vic were both first and second cousins. Their fathers, John Tapper and Tom Haskell, had married respectively Kate and Sarah, daughters of Job Rose, and their Tapper and Haskell grandfathers had married Stay sisters (since found to be daughters of John Stay).

Jim and Susie Tapper brought with them from England a large stone jar of delicious mincemeat made by Vic's mother as a present for his children. The contents lasted for months and were made into many pies, which were greatly relished by the Haskell children.

Jim Tapper was employed in Vic Haskell's railway survey party for about two years and then moved to Southland, where he became a successful farmer, eventually owning two farms. Later, as his sons were not interested in farming, he and his eldest son, Jack, ran a successful road transport carrying business. Then, at Outram, Otago, they had a service station.

When Isobel Bretherton met Jim Tapper at Outram in early 1966 his wife had died several years before and he was living with Jack. Jim told Isobel that after he and Susie went to Southland he suffered a serious injury while working in the bush with a friend. As the doctors thought he might not have long to live he and his family went home to England in 1911 for about a year and he made a remarkable recovery.

As a youth and young man Jim Tapper excelled at football and was a member of the All England Cup team. [Mrs. Bretherton thinks this may have been a schoolboy team, but is not certain.] He was also a cyclist of

66

Survey Camp near Kaikoura 1908/9
From left: Back row — Costello (camp groom), J. V. (Vic) Haskell, Bailey
Front row — Tennant (camp cook), Jim Tapper, Pierce

note and thought nothing of leaving Shaftesbury at 4 a.m. and riding to London in time for the football matches. It was through his winning a three-mile race at Blandford that he met his future wife. After he had received his medal on the dais her father, who was a friend and associate of Jim's father, introduced them.

The Tappers apparently lived to great ages. An uncle of Jim's who went to America lived to one hundred and twelve. Isobel Bretherton was also interested to hear that Vic Haskell as a baby had stayed for long periods at Tapper's. This presumably was at Burdens Farm, Twyford, in the parish of Compton Abbas, where John Tapper lived.

In 1966 when Isobel met him, Jim was planning a visit to England with his eldest daughter to see his brother and sisters. Jim was not letting them know they were coming and intended to just 'walk in'!

Doc Haskell

D'Arcy Ormonde (or Doc as he was known to all) Haskell, 1902 - 1989, became one of the Public Works Department's most distinguished civil engineers. Even as a schoolboy his teachers recognised his abilities.

For a very minor offence at the age of five he earned the displeasure of a male teacher of the stern old-fashioned sort, who approached his desk with a large strap. In a flash Doc saw the only possible way to avoid corporal punishment. Before the astonished gaze of the teacher and his sister Olive, he dropped under his desk near the back of the room and scrambled at incredible speed under all the desks of the children in front, out the door and home. Whether based on this or other evidence, the teacher afterwards remarked to Doc's father, *"Mr. Haskell, you've got a mathematical genius there!"*

Later, at Te Puke school, his teacher, Mr. Charles Bishoprick, a native of Yorkshire, apparently found him so sharp and bright in class that at roll call, instead of Doc's name, he called out, *"The Needle"*!

Doc Haskell joined the Public Works Department, at head office, Wellington, in early 1920 but soon moved to Paeroa. While in Wellington he had attended Victoria University and showed such promise that when he left the principal wrote to his father in the hope that Doc might be allowed to remain and become the college's youngest Master of Science. However, Doc was not to be diverted from his life-long ambition to be an engineer — a top engineer.

He became an engineering cadet in 1923 and spent his early years working on the difficult East Coast, North Island, railway on survey and construction work, including tunnels and viaducts, culminating in the great Mohaka viaduct. It was regarded by engineers as a masterpiece and won Doc worldwide acclaim in engineering circles. To the young engineer, however, it was like putting together the pieces of a Meccano set, *"simple enough, just a matter of putting it together"*.

There was more to it than that, however, as the Daily Telegraph, Napier, 8 December 1962, recalled at the time of Doc Haskell's retirement. Under the headline "Drama Under River", the paper related what happened at the site on the day of the great Hawke's Bay earthquake, 3 February 1931. When the earthquake struck, as Doc told his family, he tried to get out of his site office but caught his heel in the doorstep and was thrown flat on his face outside.

At the same time elsewhere in Hawke's Bay, Doc's father, Vic Haskell, and younger sister, Bess, were outdoors together but such was the terrifying power of the 'quake they were unable to remain standing, even though holding on to a fence, and Bess cried out, *"Dad! Make it stop!"*

These frightening experiences above ground, however, were as nothing compared to that endured by the men underground at the Mohaka viaduct site, as the Daily Telegraph related:

'A tense drama 70 feet below the bed of the Mohaka river on the day of the Hawke's Bay earthquake in 1931, is still a vivid memory for Mr. Haskell.

During the sinking of one of the huge concrete caissons for the foundations of the Mohaka viaduct the earthquake struck.

The caisson had to be sunk 70 feet [approximately 21.3 metres] through the bed of the river to a firm foundation. It was in the form of a huge concrete block with a steel cutting edge at the bottom and a boiler-type airlock at the top.

Through the centre of the caisson was a perpendicular shaft down which men — two at a time — went to dig out the material at the bottom and allow the caisson to sink.

To keep the water out, the interior of the caisson had to be kept under pressure and the workers had to be held in an airlock at the top to "decompress" before leaving.

When the earthquake came on February 3, two men were working down at the 70 ft. level and another man was engaged inside the airlock. The caisson heaved and lifted with the earthquake and the air escaping at the bottom allowed the water to enter.

The men below were frantic as the water poured in.

The air compressor and the power for the electric winch which lowered and raised a wire rope in the vertical tunnel were driven by an old steam engine and a belt drive.

Fortunately, the earthquake shock was along the line of the belt and not across it, and the belt stayed on the pulleys.

The man in the airlock at the top of the caisson immediately stood across the top of the shaft and prevented heavy tools from falling down the shaft on to the two men.

He then switched on the winch — was surprised to find it still working — and lowered the wire rope with its stirrup at the end down the shaft.

The two men below fought desperately to be first up and finally one came up on the rope.

"He was virtually demented with fear" recalls Mr. Haskell, *"and he made a dash to open the door to the airlocked chamber. Had he done so the three of them would have been killed.*

But Mr. Douglas Bailey (the man on duty in the airlock) seized an iron bar and struck the man down. He then laid him at the top of the shaft and sent the wire down for the second man.

When he saw his workmate had been knocked out he became calm. They waited for the "decompression" period and left the chamber — alive." '

Work on the Mohaka viaduct was suspended for several years during the Depression but resumed in 1936 and finished in record time in 1937.

The Mohaka railway viaduct, Hawke's Bay, New Zealand. Vic Haskell's son D'Arcy (Doc) was the young engineer in charge of its construction. When completed ahead of schedule in 1937 it was, at 312 feet high, 850 feet long, the highest in the southern hemisphere. (Photo by P. F. Nash, 1937)

Throughout World War II Doc Haskell headed the Aerodrome Services Branch of the Public Works Department, which was charged with the formidable task of constructing and maintaining aerodromes and seadromes and all their facilities, also radio, meteorological and coast-watching stations where needed, not only throughout New Zealand but in the 'host of islands' of the South Pacific, from Campbell Island in the south to the Gilbert and Ellice Islands in the north, from Pitcairn in the east to the New Hebrides in the west.

He and his men of the A.S.B. established and supplied these outposts with a little fleet of sailing vessels with auxiliary engines, which plied the great ocean often loaded to the gunwales. They were frequently called on to assist the American forces.

71

The schooner Tagua, one of Doc Haskell's wartime fleet, photographed by him at Rarotonga

Early in 1941, when the German pocket battleship Admiral Scheer was expected to refuel near the sub-Antarctic Campbell and Auckland Islands, Doc was given just ten days to establish coast-watching stations on the bleak and uninhabited islands, and did it. This was the highly secret Cape Expedition, later scientific members of which named a place in the Auckland Islands as Haskell Bay *"after the old man"*, as Doc put it!

On 22 November 1941, at the request of the Americans (fifteen days before the Japanese attack on Pearl Harbour on 7 December), Doc was ordered to upgrade the grass airfield at Nandi, Fiji to take heavy bombers and transport planes by 15 January 1942. This was to provide a vital air link between America and Australia, New Zealand and the South Pacific islands. In this emergency Doc reacted by commandeering a passenger ship and gathering 440 men and machinery from all over New Zealand and landing them in Fiji on 30 November. More followed, and by working night and day and doing in days what normally took weeks they had the first runway ready for three Flying Fortresses to land on 10 January 1942, five days ahead of schedule. In the New Zealand official history of the war in the Pacific it is stated that the successful completion of the Nandi project was one of New Zealand's most important achievements in the Pacific theatre of war.

Doc and his men had more than enough practical difficulties getting bulldozers ashore at islands and hewing aerodromes and seadromes out of coral rock, coconut plantations and mangrove swamps, but even in the midst of a world war the local population could hold up some vital construction work.

New Zealand needed an aerodrome at Norfolk Island as an important link with the islands to the north of it. However, Norfolk Island was administered by Australia, and Doc was strictly instructed by the New Zealand Prime Minister not to argue with the civil authorities there. However, the only possible site for an airstrip was occupied by a magnificent row of pines, and very strong local opposition would not permit their destruction. It took all the diplomatic skills of the American admirals Nimitz and Halsey to allow the work to proceed in 1942, the year in which the Japanese drove into the South Pacific.

As a qualified pilot, Doc flew himself about the Pacific until, as he said, he *"became a little too valuable to the Department"*. He also sailed in his little ships and once nearly lost his life when one of them was wrecked in a typhoon. His men, too, faced danger and death.

D'Arcy (Doc) Haskell

(This photograph and the previous one of the schooner Tagua are reproduced from the book Airline by kind permission of the author, Ian Driscoll)

Those at Suwarrow had to take refuge in a crow's nest at the top of a tree when their atoll was completely submerged in a hurricane. Some of the coast watchers captured by the Japanese in the Gilbert Islands, who had volunteered to send radio reports till the last, were cruelly treated and later publicly executed.

After the war Doc eventually became Commissioner of Works in the district where he had begun his career — the Hawke's Bay/Gisborne district, East Coast, North Island. After his retirement in 1962 he devoted his energies to various local authorities to which he was elected, and was awarded the M.B.E. in 1968 for his services in this regard.

In the Parliamentary general election of 1963 Doc Haskell contested the safe Labour seat of Napier, Hawke's Bay, for the National Party, and reduced substantially the sitting member's majority. He ran a good-humoured campaign and found while canvassing for votes that every call on householders was a pleasant one. As Commissioner of Works he had known the Labour Member, Jim Edwards, so he *"called for a cup of tea and a chat when in his part of town"*!

From his longstanding interest in the welfare of the working men and their families, it surprised many that he stood against the Labour Party. Indeed, one of his relations once proclaimed, *"Doc's a Red!"* Recalling the campaign, Doc laughed when he said that a waterside worker grabbed him *"by the scruff"* and demanded, *"What do you mean by deserting us!"*

At the time of his retirement late in 1962 the Daily Telegraph, Napier, remarked that his career had been one of the most colourful in the Ministry of Works: 'During his 43 years he has worked in the air, on the ground, under the ground, on the water and under the water. He has helped to survey, plan and build railways, roads, bridges, tunnels, a hydro-electric scheme, aerodromes, river and harbour works, and water supplies. He has ridden and driven horses and every conceivable vehicle from a push cycle to a railway engine. He has piloted aeroplanes; sailed and navigated ships . . . . With his department, Mr. Haskell at times gained a reputation for disregard of rules, but he has always been anxious to get work done . . . . During his career he has made many friends and few, if any, enemies. He has been able to talk on even terms with everyone from Governor-Generals to dustmen and, as he says, has 'found similar qualities in all'.'

The Hawke's Bay Herald Tribune, describing him as "physically a slight figure, a man you would pass in a crowd", praised not only his ability to get things done in the public interest but his openness about his department's doings and his diplomatic ability: "There has been many an incipient row stopped while he has been in the chair. His friendly manner, his thorough grasp of all the facts, and his ability to put them across clearly, has been one of his greatest assets."

75

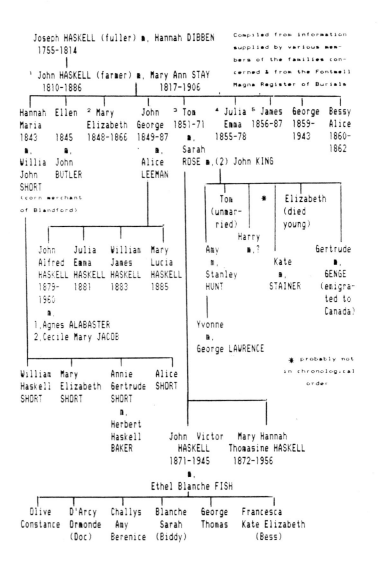

Joseph HASKELL (fuller) m, Hannah DIBBEN
1755-1814

1 John HASKELL (farmer) m, Mary Ann STAY
1810-1886   1817-1906

Compiled from information supplied by various members of the families concerned & from the Fontmell Magna Register of Burials

Hannah Ellen — 2 Mary — John — 3 Tom — 4 Julia — 5 James — George — Bessy
Maria / Elizabeth / George / 1851-71 / Emma / 1856-87 / 1859- / Alice
1843 1845 1848-1866 1849-87 m, Sarah ROSE m,(2) John KING 1855-78 1943 1860-1862
m, Willia John SHORT (corn merchant of Blandford)
m, John BUTLER
m, Alice LEEMAN

Tom (unmarried)   *   Elizabeth (died young)
Harry

John Alfred HASKELL 1879-1960 / Julia Emma HASKELL 1881 / William James HASKELL 1883 / Mary Lucia HASKELL 1885
m, 1,Agnes ALABASTER 2,Cecile Mary JACOB

Amy m, Stanley HUNT
Yvonne m, George LAWRENCE

m,? Kate m, STAINER

Gertrude m, GENGE (emigrated to Canada)

* probably not in chronological order

William Haskell SHORT / Mary Elizabeth SHORT / Annie Gertrude SHORT m, Herbert Haskell BAKER / Alice SHORT

John Victor HASKELL 1871-1945 — Mary Hannah Thomasine HASKELL 1872-1956
m, Ethel Blanche FISH

Olive Constance / D'Arcy Ormonde (Doc) / Challys Amy Berenice / Blanche Sarah (Biddy) / George Thomas / Francesca Kate Elizabeth (Bess)

Footnote: (Entries in Burial Register, Fontmell Magna)
1 John Haskell buried Fontmell Magna 3 February 1886. Age 75
   Mary Ann (nee Stay) Haskell (abode Iwerne Minster) buried Fontmell Magna 14 February 1906. Age 89
2 Mary Elizabeth Haskell buried Fontmell Magna 5 January 1866. Age 18
3 Tom Haskell (abode Compton Abbas) buried Fontmell Magna 4 April 1872. Age 20
4 Julia Emma Haskell buried Fontmell Magna 1 July 1878. Age 24
5 James Haskell buried Fontmell Magna 30 March 1887. Age 30

To admiring relations who remarked on his outstanding career, Doc Haskell would respond modestly that he had been lucky to be chosen for his big engineering works, and as to his wartime achievements, he passed them off with *"I was just one of the team"*.

George Haskell

Doc Haskell's younger brother, George, a marine engineer, also carried out valuable work for the Allied cause in World War II. After being commended by the British Consul for his work for the defence of Tonga as seadrome engineer and with the island's land and sea transport, he returned to New Zealand to work on experimental weapons testing with Colonel Basil Grove (or Groves), who apparently came from the Dorset/Wiltshire area. After the war George Haskell became a successful farmer.

Printed sources: ⁄

Aerodrome Services Branch, P.W.D., Official War History (unpublished)

Airline . . . Ian Driscoll, 1979

The Pacific, Official History of New Zealand in the Second World War 1939-45
O. A. Gillespie, 1952

By Design, A Brief History of the Public Works Department 1870-1970
Rosslyn J. Noonan, 1975

Various newspaper reports   ,,

*   *   *   *   *   *   *   *   *   *

[This is the end of the contribution from New Zealand by Olive and Alister Matheson and Isobel Bretherton]

*   *   *   *   *   *   *   *   *   *

KATE

Kate, Job Rose's fourth daughter, was born in June 1854 and baptised at Fontmell Magna. In 1878 she married Henry John Tapper (known as John), who farmed at Burdens Farm, Twyford (Compton Abbas). He and his brother-in-law Tom Rose were life-long friends and fellow Wesleyan Methodists. The

77

villages in which they lived and farmed were not far from each other, and the two families seem to have enjoyed a close and warm relationship.

John Tapper was active in the community, and an entry in the 1911 edition of Kelly's Directory includes the following entry: "Tapper John, farmer, & registrar of births & deaths, Fontmell sub-district, Shaftesbury union, Burden's farm". He was also the Councillor for Compton Abbas in the Shaftesbury Rural District Council for many years.

Kate Rose and John Tapper when engaged

John and Kate Tapper had five children — two sons, James (Jim) and William and three daughters, Geraldine, Elizabeth (Bess) and Kate (Kitty).

John Tapper (with dark horse) in front of Burdens Farm, Twyford

In 1919, on his retirement, John Tapper bought Woodbridge Mill and he and Kate went there to live. When their eldest daughter Geraldine was widowed, in the 1930's, she too made Woodbridge her home. Although only a child when her grandmother died, Anne Barnes remembers Kate Tapper as *"a very determined old lady, either in bed or a wheelchair"*.

79

L. to r. James (Jim), Geraldine, William
Elizabeth (Bess), John Tapper, Kate (Kitty), Kate Tapper (nee Rose)
Photo 1903

Woodbridge Mill, early, 1900's

Photograph which appeared in a booklet published in 1928 by the Shaftesbury/
Gillingham Circuit of the Wesleyan Methodist Church, with the following article:

81

Golden Wedding. 1878--April 24th--1928. Jubilee of Service at Hartgrove Wesleyan Church.

Mr. John Tapper, of Twyford, and Miss Kate Rose, of Bedchester, were married at the Gillingham Wesleyan Church on April 24th, 1878.

Mr. Tapper was formerly a Sunday School Teacher in the Parish Church of Compton Abbas where Mr. Frank Miller, now at Bourton, was one of his boys. Evidently Mrs. Tapper was of the stronger mind, for Mr. Tapper joined the Hartgrove Wesleyan Church when he was married. He became immediately associated with the Sunday School, succeeding Mr. Tom Rose as Superintendent, which position Mr. Tapper still holds. He has also occupied every position open to a Methodist Layman.

Mr. Job Rose, father of Mrs. Tapper, was for many years a strong supporter of the Hartgrove Wesleyan Church. One of his daughters was organist till her marriage to Mr. James Herridge, when Miss Kate Rose took over the duties. During the early years of their marriage Mr. Tapper played the organ until their eldest daughter—now Mrs. Edwards— was old enough to occupy the stool. Mrs. Edwards was succeeded by her younger sister who held the position till her marriage to Mr. Hart. The position of organist was thus held by the family for sixty years.

There are five children. Mrs. Edwards, wife of the Rev. H. W. Edwards, of Fontmell Magna, now at Leicester; Mrs. L. B. Clarke, of Putney; Mrs. A. K. Hart, of Birmingham;—both husbands are circuit stewards. The eldest son has been in New Zealand for twenty years and is a keen supporter of the Church. The second son, Rev. William Tapper, is a Wesleyan Minister at Putney.

Throughout their married life Mr. and Mrs. Tapper have been Leaders of the Hartgrove Society, and have entertained the preachers on Sundays.

They celebrated their golden wedding at their home at Woodbridge, which was formerly the home of Mr. Job Rose. It was here that Mr. Tapper did his courting, and I have heard that Miss Kate Rose used to frequent a favourite walk down by the little stream presumably to pick forget-me-nots, but really to meet her John. May they be spared many years to stroll over the familiar and hallowed ground. Innumerable friends join in heartiest congratulations to Mr. and Mrs. Tapper, and Praise to God for their work and influence.

82

(1) Jack Edwards (2) Ernest Clarke (3) Geraldine (4) William Tapper (5) Kingsley Hart
(6) Mrs. Hart (7) Emma May Tapper (8) John Tapper (9) Elizabeth (10) Kate
(11) Josephine
(12) Patricia June (13) Dr. Geoffrey Tapper (14) Ann Clarke
Photograph 1936

1. Jack, son of Geraldine and Rev. Harry Edwards, Fontmell Magna
2. Ernest Clarke, husband of Elizabeth (Bess), middle daughter of John and Kate Tapper
3. Geraldine, eldest daughter of John and Kate Tapper
4. William Tapper, son of John and Kate Tapper. Army Chaplain 1914-1918, Methodist Minister
5. Kingsley Hart, husband of Kate (Kitty), youngest daughter of John and Kate Tapper. Birmingham ironmonger
6. Kingsley's mother — 'old Mrs. Hart'
7. Emma May, wife of the Rev. William Tapper
8. John Tapper, husband of Kate, nee Rose. Farmed at Burden's Farm, Twyford (Compton Abbas) until retirement. Bought Woodbridge at Glyn sale in 1919 and lived there until death of his wife Kate and his daughter Geraldine, then a widow
9. Elizabeth (Bess) middle daughter of John and Kate Tapper. Wife of Ernest Clarke
10. Kate (Kitty) youngest daughter of John and Kate Tapper. Wife of Kingsley Hart
11. Josephine (Jo), daughter of Kinglsey and Kitty Hart. Married Peter Stammers, a laundry owner in Fulham SW

83

12. Patricia June (known as June), daughter of William and Emma May Tapper
13. Dr. Geoffrey Tapper of Shaftesbury, son of William and Emma May Tapper
14. Anne, daughter of Ernest & Bess Clarke. Married a naval officer (whose family is believed to have a connection with William Barnes)

Kate Tapper spent the last two or three years of her life in a wheelchair. Following her death (in January 1936 at the age of 81) and that of Geraldine, John Tapper went to live with his second daughter Bess in Putney, London S.W. He remained there from 1946 until his death on 9 November 1949, when he was 94 years old. He and his wife are both buried at Fontmell Magna.

Jim (the second child and elder son of John and Kate Tapper) was born in May 1882, and emigrated to New Zealand in 1906.

His relatives in New Zealand have supplied some information about him, which appears on Page 66 in the section about Sarah Rose. Anne Barnes (nee Clarke) — Jim's niece — has written: *"Jim had six children — Jack, Phyllis, Charles, Bill (now dead), Jim and Mary. All except Jim have visited us at some time.*

Bill and Jim were both in the New Zealand Navy during the war, but only Bill came to the U.K. Charles was in the R.A.F. and won the D.F.C. My mother and I went with him to the Palace when he received it."

Jim Tapper obviously made the proposed trip to Britain to see his brother and sisters, which he had discussed with Isobel Bretherton in New Zealand in 1966. Mrs. Barnes continues: *"Uncle Jim came to Guernsey with his daughter Phyllis to visit us and my mother in 1966 . . . . . My mother was worried that she wouldn't recognise him after so many years. However, he was so like John Tapper, her father, in looks, mannerisms and even had a Dorset accent, that my Mother called him 'Dad' throughout his visit."*

JACK AND IVOR FRANCIS

Ivor Francis [1908 - 1991]

For many years until the west wing was demolished in 1956, the main part of what is now Fiddleford Mill House consisted of three cottages and a stable. [Page 36 W.E.T.G.]   Jack Francis lived in one of these cottages and worked on the farm as an agricultural labourer for Mr. Sidney Rose, who also leased the Mill. Ivor, son of Jack Francis, was an employee of Blandford and Webb, and also lived in Fiddleford.

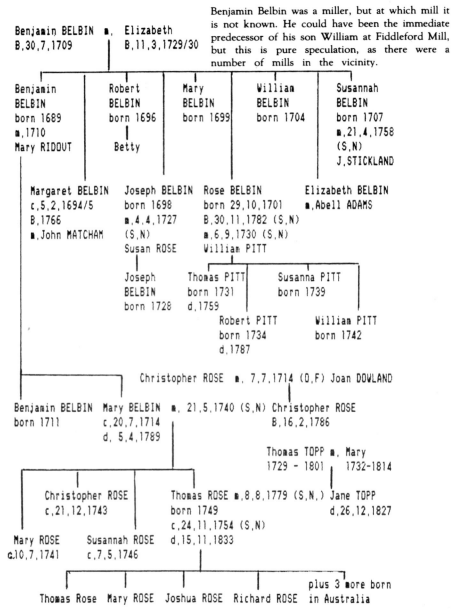

Benjamin Belbin was a miller, but at which mill it is not known. He could have been the immediate predecessor of his son William at Fiddleford Mill, but this is pure speculation, as there were a number of mills in the vicinity.

Benjamin BELBIN ■, Elizabeth
B,30,7,1709   B,11,3,1729/30

Benjamin   Robert   Mary   William   Susannah
BELBIN   BELBIN   BELBIN   BELBIN   BELBIN
born 1689   born 1696   born 1699   born 1704   born 1707
■,1710   ■,21,4,1758
Mary RIDOUT   Betty   (S,N)
                                                                  J,STICKLAND

Margaret BELBIN   Joseph BELBIN   Rose BELBIN   Elizabeth BELBIN
c,5,2,1694/5   born 1698   born 29,10,1701   ■,Abell ADAMS
B,1766   ■,4,4,1727   B,30,11,1782 (S,N)
■,John MATCHAM   (S,N)   ■,6,9,1730 (S,N)
                      Susan ROSE   William PITT

                      Joseph   Thomas PITT   Susanna PITT
                      BELBIN   born 1731   born 1739
                      born 1728   d,1759
                                              Robert PITT   William PITT
                                              born 1734   born 1742
                                              d,1787

                  Christopher ROSE ■, 7,7,1714 (O,F) Joan DOWLAND

Benjamin BELBIN   Mary BELBIN   ■, 21,5,1740 (S,N) Christopher ROSE
born 1711   c,20,7,1714   B,16,2,1786
                  d, 5,4,1789

                                        Thomas TOPP ■, Mary
                                        1729 - 1801   1732-1814

          Christopher ROSE   Thomas ROSE ■,8,8,1779 (S,N,) Jane TOPP
          c,21,12,1743   born 1749   d,26,12,1827
                                c,24,11,1754 (S,N)
Mary ROSE   Susannah ROSE d,15,11,1833
c.10,7,1741   c,7,5,1746

                                                        plus 3 more born
          Thomas Rose   Mary ROSE   Joshua ROSE   Richard ROSE in Australia

Family line compiled from information supplied
by Barbara Lamble, Kenneth Topp & other sources

86

THE INNS OF FIDDLEFORD

THE TROUT, THE FISH and MAY COTTAGE

A lease in respect of May Cottage has cast new light on the history of the house. When Where Elm Trees Grew was published four years ago there seemed to be no sure way of discovering anything about the cottage itself or its inhabitants prior to 1841/2 (the time of the Tithe Map and that year's general Census).

The dating of the house as *"late 18th century"* by the Royal Commission in its publication Historical Monuments in the County of Dorset suggested that there might be only fifty years or so before 1841 to research. However, it seemed obvious that parts of the house were much older than the Royal Commission had stated.

The Indenture [D.C.R.O. D.PIT/T341] which revealed more about the premises was a contract between George Pitt Esq. of Stratfieldsea and Robert Pitt of Fiddleford, yeoman, which followed the surrender of a previous lease dated 8 May 1759 (same property) in the names of William Belbin of Fiddleford, and Joseph Belbin, his nephew.

The new Indenture (dated 12 May 1766) granted to Robert Pitt (nephew of William Belbin) a lease of *"all that cottage or dwellinghouse commonly called or known by the name of the Trout Alehouse together with a Garden and Orchard to the same belonging containing in the whole by estimation one acre be the same more or less, all which premises are situate lying and being in ffiddleford aforesaid within the Manor of Belchalwell in the said county of Dorset . . . . . "*

The lease includes *"all ways paths passages priviledges and advantages whatsoever to the said Cottage or Dwellinghouse"* except *"all manner of Timber and other Trees Slips and Young Saplings growing or to grow on the premises and the Royalty and all casual profits happening thereon."*

87

The rent was ten shillings [50p] payable on 29 September and 25 March each year. There was a fine of 3/4d [17p] in any case of default, and Robert Pitt was to *"well and sufficiently repair maintain support amend and keep the premises and every part thereof in all and all manner of needful and necessary reparations and amendments whatsoever . . . . . "*

The words *"cottage or dwellinghouse commonly called or known by the name of the Trout Alehouse . . . . in Fiddleford aforesaid within the Manor of Belchalwell"* were exciting because May Cottage was the ONLY house in Fiddleford which was in the Manor of Belchalwell. It is virtually certain, therefore, that for some time in the 18th century May Cottage must have been an alehouse.

Other factors, if any were needed, which support May Cottage as the location are:

(1) it was traditionally listed as having a garden and orchard which covered an acre of land

(2) it was customary for the occupant of May Cottage to be a *"woodman"* (see Census Returns 1841 — Joseph Jeans; 1881 — Job Ridout) and on the front of the 1766 (folded) lease are the words *"Belchalwell — Woodmans House"*.

This was a surprising discovery, and it was therefore rather disappointing to find that the Registers of Alehouse Recognizances failed to disclose any record of The Trout in either Belchalwell or Fiddleford. However, it was quite commonplace for names of premises not to be given — most of the entries consisted only of the licensee and the parish. But one name — The Fish at Belchalwell — did appear several times. (Belchalwell entries in the Registers are listed at the end of this section).

Since in the Registers there is only one entry per year for Belchalwell, there must have been only one alehouse. It might have been expected that this would have been in the main part of the village, some three or four miles from Fiddleford, but that could not be the case if the entries refer to May Cottage.

Another puzzle is that the document of 1766 mentions The Trout Alehouse in Fiddleford/Belchalwell, but the only name referred to in the Alehouse Registers that year is The Fish in Belchalwell. Were The Trout and The Fish one and the same?

To try to solve the mystery it might be appropriate to start with William Pitt, who held a licence for premises in Fiddleford in 1748 and 1749. He died in December 1749 and his widow Rose carried on the business, presumably in the same house, between 1750 and 1752. The Register records that this was in Fiddleford/Okeford Fitzpaine. It was, in fact, The Bell (later The Travellers Rest).

William Dawson took over The Bell in 1753, so before that date Rose Pitt must have gone to another address. It seems probable that all her children would still be living with her, as they were unmarried and only one was over twenty years of age. Did she and her family move to May Cottage?

It was in 1752 that Rose Pitt's eldest son, Thomas, had his twenty-first birthday (the minimum age at which one could legally become a licensee). In the same year he was granted a licence for premises in Belchalwell. Rose, with her previous experience in the trade, would have been able to help her son.

We know that (with the exception of two years) Thomas Pitt had licensed premises in Belchalwell from 1752 until 1758, and, after his death in May 1759 at the age of twenty-seven, his mother Rose Pitt carried on with the licence. She appears in the Registers until 1770, and, as this is the last date for which the D.C.R.O. has records of Alehouse Recognizances, she may have been there for some years after 1770.

So it is established that the Pitts had an alehouse in Belchalwell for at least eighteen years. The unfortunate thing is that the Registers do not give the exact location — the only clue is that several entries refer to "The Fish in Belchalwell".

Now consider firm evidence from the 1766 Lease. Tenancy of The Trout in Fiddleford/Belchalwell was granted to William Belbin on 8 May 1759. Was it just chance that the date of this lease was only two days after his nephew, Thomas Pitt, licensee of The Fish in Belchalwell, was buried on 6 May 1759?

It could, of course, be that these were two entirely different premises, and the fact that the dates coincide might be completely irrelevant. But it seems much more likely that Thomas Pitt held the lease of The Fish until his death, when it passed to his uncle, William Belbin. If this is the case, then:

(1) The Fish and The Trout were one and the same
(2) As the Deed proves that The Trout was, in fact, what is now called May Cottage, The Fish must also have been at May Cottage
(3) In 1752 Thomas Pitt acquired the lease of, as well as a licence for, May Cottage, and Rose Belbin and the rest of her family moved there with him from The Bell Inn

Further support for this theory is the fact that it was in 1766 that Robert Pitt took over the lease of The Trout from his uncle William Belbin. It was also in 1766 that Robert Pitt first signed as one of the two Recognizances for his mother Rose Pitt, then the licensee of The Fish. Although it would be quite feasible for Robert to act as surety for his mother if she carried on her business in premises in which he had no personal interest, it seems much more likely that she was, in fact, in the cottage for which he held the lease.

If this is correct, why do the Registers refer to The Fish when the lease calls the property The Trout Alehouse? Perhaps the name was changed at some time, or, as the Deed records, the cottage was "commonly called or known by the name of The Trout Alehouse . ."

Freak entries do nothing to help solve the puzzle. An example is 1759, when the entry in the Alehouse Registers shows "Rose Pitt of Sturminster Newton Castle". This was the one occasion when the licence was applied for at Stalbridge, and the reference to Sturminster Newton Castle was probably a mistake, as for the following ten years when the applications were made at Shaston (Shaftesbury) Rose Pitt is again shown as "of Belchalwell".

It would also be interesting to know how long there had been an alehouse at May Cottage before it was mentioned in the 1766 lease. In 1714 John Churchill's name appears twice:

(1) at Shaston, as one of two recognizances for Robert Willis of East Orchard — *"John Churchill of Bell Chalwell"*

(2) in the same month at Sturminster Newton Castle, where he applied for his own licence — *"John Churchill of ffittleford"*.

Assuming that these two entries refer to the same man, this suggests that his address was Fiddleford/Belchalwell, in which case there must have been an inn at May Cottage as far back as 1714.

Some of this chapter is, through lack of written evidence, pure speculation. The connection between The Trout Alehouse (May Cottage) and The Fish is something which probably will never be established. On balance, the facts which are available lead one to think that they were the same premises. But unless more documents come to light, this cannot be verified.

One irrefutable fact is that THERE WAS at some time during the 18th century an alehouse called The Trout at May Cottage, Fiddleford in the Manor of Belchalwell . . . . the Indenture of 1766 proves this.

Appendix 2 of *Where Elm Trees Grew* gives the licensees shown in the Registers as *"Fiddleford"*. The following entries are listed as *"Belchalwell"* or have some connection with Belchalwell licensees:

	Sessions at:
1714 Robert Willis of East Orchard	Shaston
Recognizances: John Churchill of Bell Chalwell and one other	
1714 John Churchill of ffittleford	Stur. Newton Castle
1715	
1716	
1717	
1718 Maria Hustis of Bell Challwell victr	Gillingham
1719 Maria Hustis of Belchalwell	Shaston
1720	
1721 Anna Husten of Bell Chalwell	Stur. Newton Castle

1722		
1723		
1724	Anna Huston of Belchalwell	Blandford Forum
	(one recognizance in the name of John Huston	
	of Dewlish, maltster)	
1725	Anna Hustons of Belchalwell	Shaston
1726	Anna Huston of Bel Chalwell	Stur. Newton Castle
1727	Anne Hustings Bellchalwell	Wimborne (Cashmore)
1728	Anna Hustings of Belchalwell	Stur. Newton Castle
1729	Anna Hustings of Bel Chalwell	Shaston
1730	Anna Hustings of Bel Chalwell	Shaston
1731		
1732	Willus Trowbridge of Belchalwell	Shaston
1733	William Trowbridge of Belchalwell (plus brandy)	Shaston
1734		
1735		
1736	William Trowbridge of Belchalwell	Shaston
1737	William Trowbridge of Belchalwell	Stur. Newton Castle
1738	William Trowbridge of Belchalwell	Shaston
1739	William Trowbridge of Belchalwell	Shaston
1740	William Trowbridge of Belchalwell	Shaston
1741		
1742	William Trowbridge of Belchalwell	Shaston
1743	Wm. Trowbridge of Bellchallwell	Shaston
1744	William Gould of Belchalwell	Stur. Newton Castle
1745	Wm. Gould of Bellchalwell	Shaston
1746	William Gould of Bellchalwell	Shaston
1747		
1748	Wm. Pitt of Fidelford	Stur. Newton Castle
1749	Wm. Pitt of Fidleford	Stur. Newton Castle
1750	Rose Pitt of [Fiddletord deleted]	
	Okeford Fitzpain widow	Stur. Newton Castle
1751	Rose Pitt of Okeford Fitzpain	Stur. Newton Castle
1752	Thomas Pitt of Belchallwell	Shaston
1753	Thomas Pitt at the Sign of the Fish in Bellchalwell	Stur. New. Castle
1754		
1755	William Gould of Belchalwell	Stur. Newton Castle
1756	Thomas Pit of Bellchallwell	Shaston
1757	Thomas Pitt of Bellchalwell	Shaston
1758	Thomas Pitt of Belchalwell	Shaston
1759	Rose Pitt at the Fish in Sturminster Newton Castle	Stalbridge
1760	Rose Pitt of Belchalwell widow	Shaston
1761	Rose Pitt of Belchalwell	Shaston
1762	Rose Pitt	Shaston
1763	Rose Pitt of Belchalwell widow	Shaston

1764 Rose	Pitt	of	Belchalwell	widow		Shaston
1765 Rose	Pitt	of	Belchalwell	widow		Shaston
1766 Rose	Pitt	at the Fish in	Belchalwell	widow		Shaston
1767 Rose	Pitt	at the Fish in	Belchalwell			Shaston
1768 Rose	Pitt	at the Fish in	Belchalwell	widow		Shaston
1769 Rose	Pitt	of	Belchalwell	widow		Shaston
1770 Rose	Pitt	of	Bellchalwell	victr		Shaston

THE BELL INN

In 1753 William Dawson became licensee at The Bell Inn, Fiddleford, and he was still there in 1770, recorded in the last of the Registers of Alehouse Recognizances at the Dorset County Records Office.

In 1821, Philip Adams applied for a licence to *"keep a certain common inn or Alehouse at Ockford Fitzpaine known by the sign of the Travellers Rest . . . . . "*

It is interesting that a lease of 1824 which grants Philip Adams the premises *". . . . . formerly called the Bell Public House but now the Travellers Rest"* includes 'three lives', the first being *"Samuel Dawson aged sixty-one or thereabouts"*. It is virtually certain that this was Samuel, son of William and Hannah Dawson, baptised at Okeford Fitzpaine in April 1760.

But what happened between 1770 and 1821? William Dawson died in 1786. Did his son Samuel continue to live there, and did he carry on as licensee?

Mr. H. L. Douch of Truro, Cornwall, whose relative lived at the Travellers Rest a hundred years or so after these events took place, has supplied the following information:

"I have been scouring the advertisement columns of the Sherborne Mercury; suddenly the name of Fiddleford jumped out at me. The advert appeared on February 19th 1810 and in the following week. There was to be a sale at the Swan Inn, Sturminster Newton, by order of the assignees of Samuel Dawson, bankrupt, of:—

93

'Lot 1. All that Messuage or Dwelling-House called the Bell Inn, with the Barn, Barton, Stables, Garden and Orchard containing about 3 acres (more or less) situate at Fiddleford, and adjoining the public road from that place and Sturminster to Blandford.

Lot 2. A Close of exceeding Rich Meadow Land called Cummerwick, containing, by estimation 8 acres (more or less) adjoining the road leading from Fiddleford to Okeford Fitzpaine.

Lot 3. A Dwelling-House, Garden, two Orchards and two small Closes of Meadow Land containing, in the whole, about 3 acres (more or less) adjoining the back road leading from Lot 1 to Fiddleford Mills.

Lot 4. An excellent Close of Meadow Land, divided from the last lot by a stream of water, containing 3 acres (more or less).

Lot 5. The Beneficial Interest of the Assignees, in a contract entered into by the said Bankrupt, for the purchase of a Close of Meadow Land called Breach Mead, containing by admeasurement 3A. OR. 10P. near the road leading from Sturminster to Fiddleford aforesaid and lately in the occupation of Mr. Isaac.

All the above Premises are held for the lives of healthy persons, under Lord Rivers, are in the parishes of Sturminster Newton, and Okeford Fitzpaine aforesaid (except Lot 5) and were lately occupied by the said Bankrupt. Possession of the whole will be given at Lady-day next.

Immediately after the sale will be LET by AUCTION three SMALL ESTATES, rented by the Bankrupt, called Duck Lane, Gasses and Leighs, all situate in the parish of Sturminster Newton . . . .

On the same day at eleven o'clock in the forenoon in the Market Place at Sturminster Newton aforesaid will be SOLD in lots the STOCK and FARMING UTENSILS of the said Bankrupt, consisting of cart and saddle horses, cows, waggons, and a dung pot, with harness, saddles, bridles etc.

For viewing the lands apply to Thomas Davidge at the Bell Inn aforesaid, and other particulars may be had of Mr. Kaines at

Manston (one of the Assignees); of Mr. Score, solicitor, Sherborne; and of Mr. George Score, solicitor, Sturminster Newton aforesaid.'

The sale was to take place on March 1st."

Mr. Douch says that he found two more references to Samuel Dawson in the Sherborne Mercury. "They are notices of meetings of his creditors: in them he is described as 'jobber in bullocks, dealer and chapman', any one of which occupations might have led him into bankruptcy." [A chapman is a pedlar or hawker].

Presumably The Bell Inn was sold in 1810. Was it still being used as a Public House?

To what place	Date when sent	Stamps

CHOBHAM · YATELY · ASH · FRIMLEY · THORPE · FIDDLEFORD · GREAT-BARFORD · MAGDALEN-STREET · ST-STEPHEN'S-GATES · ST-GILES'S · NEWTON-PICNEY · BRONLLY'S · WEAVERHAM · HARTFORD · ((925))

Post Office Steel Impression Book   Vol. 14.   Page 205
from Post Office Archives

96

THE POST OFFICE

Miss Betty Savage of Poole and Mr. M. O. Welch of Bridgwater (Secretary) of The Somerset and Dorset Postal History Group have been helpful in supplying some interesting information about the Sub-Post Office at Fiddleford, although unfortunately the name of the first Sub-Postmaster remains a mystery.

A submission for a post office was made on 23 March 1858 and a month later, on 22 April 1858 an undated circular hand-stamp was issued to Fiddleford.

"The design of undated circular marks can be traced back to the circular mileage marks of the late 1700's and early 1800's. When the figures of mileage were removed in the 1820's it was a simple matter of design to replace the figures with double arcs and thus these now very interesting and collectable marks were born. With certain exceptions offices of any status with an annual revenue of less than £1000 were issued with undated handstamps but by 1840 nearly all principal offices in Post Towns, regardless of the amount of revenue, had been issued with dated circular handstamps in replacement of their undated stamps.

By far the largest number of undated circular marks included in this study were issued to Post Towns during the 1840's and 1850's for use at their subordinate offices. The background to this situation lies in the proposal made by the Postmaster General to the Secretary, Colonel W. L. Maberley, that every receiver should have a stamp bearing the name of his or her office which he or she could strike on every letter received at the office. This suggestion was adopted . . . . As new rural or other minor offices were opened they were issued with an undated circular mark."

These varied in diameter, until, from a standard 29mm. in the mid 1830's they were reduced to 25mm. in 1844 and from 1857 they gradually became still smaller until the later types were 19mm. across.

"Undated circular marks were issued to identify the place of posting of a letter and were not to be used for cancelling adhesives. The 1853 Rules for Postmasters state that the impression of the handstamp must be placed on the back of paid letters. It is clear, however, that in Somerset and Dorset this rule was not always observed as there are many examples of handstamps being struck on the front of letters . . . . . Some village offices also struck their mark on the reverse of incoming letters by way of a receiving mark. It is possible therefore to see two, three or possibly more different marks on one letter."

"The stamping of letters at all offices using undated handstamps came to an end in 1860 after the issue of an Instruction to Postmasters dated 17 March in that year. By then, many letters were being posted in letter boxes and the identification of the place of posting was less relevant. Additionally the attraction of the subsequent reduction in costs clearly appealed to the Post Office . . . . . . ''

[The preceding information is from The Undated Circular Marks of Somerset and Dorset - Editors John H. Millener and Betty Savage, published by the Somerset & Dorset Postal History Group ISSN 0950   2874]

Mr. Welch says that after the withdrawal of the undated postmarks in March 1860, "a small office like Fiddleford would have **no** handstamp until it was allowed to sell Postal Orders — sometime after 1885. (Mail would be cancelled at the Head Office.)

If it became a 'Money Order Office' i.e. allowed to sell M.O.s it would have been issued with a dated steel handstamp. The fact that it received a rubber handstamp in 1904 suggests it was never of M.O.O. status — although there is a slight possibility that it had been such for a time and then down-graded again.

A rubber handstamp for dating postal orders was sent 23 March 1904.

Soon after this, village offices were allowed to use them to cancel mail also. It may not be the first such handstamp, because proof strikes in the Record Books were not 100%, although this early they were still very thorough . . . . . . It was at this time — mid 1904 — that all remaining offices were allowed to sell postal orders, and I suspect this was one such office.

Such rubber handstamps did not last long . . . . . . Remember they often used the wrong type of ink which could cause damage and swelling of the rubber — you have to allow for this . . . . ."

Although, as Mr. Welch says, these were not long-lasting, a postcard posted at Fiddleford on 10 July 1912 bears a mark from the rubber handstamp issued in 1904.

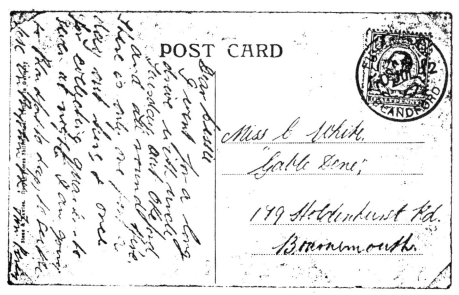

reproduced by permission of Miss Betty Savage

Miss Savage has also provided copies of two double ring handstamps with the following comments:

"The type used in 1933 had short thick bars separating the village name from the post town and county names — BLANDFORD DORSET. Note that the day plugs are inverted '22'.

The handstamp of 1954 has large dots instead of the thick bars of the earlier type. Note STURMINSTER NEWTON. DST."

reproduced by permission of Miss Betty Savage

The following excerpts (supplied by Miss Savage) from Kelly's Directories show that a 'potted' history of the Post Offices can be obtained from these volumes:

In Kelly's 1859 edition the office was listed under Sturminster Newton. "Letters through Sturminster Newton, which is the nearest Money Order Office."

In 1890 (under Okeford Fitzpaine) the entry reads "George Adams, receiver. Letters from Blandford arrive at 6.15 a.m.; dispatched at 6.40 p.m. The nearest money order and telegraph offices are at Shillingstone and Sturminster Newton."

James Ridout was the sub-Postmaster in 1903. Letters arrived and were despatched at the same times and the nearest money order and telegraph office was at Sturminster Newton "3 miles distant".

1915 — "Mrs. Harriet Louisa Ridout, sub Postmistress. Letters from Blandford via Sturminster Newton arrive at 7.30 a.m.;

despatched at 6.40 p.m. Sturminster Newton, 2½ miles distant is the nearest money order and telegraph office."

1939 — "Post Office, Fiddleford. Letters through Blandford. Sturminster Newton nearest money order and telegraph office. Jas. Hilliar Ridout, grocer and post office. Sturminster Newton 65 [tel. no.]"

Harriet Ridout and her son Fred (c. 1907)

On Page 137 of **Where Elm Trees Grew** is a picture of Bill Earle and the three Rose boys, with an anonymous small child. What a thrill it was to receive a letter and photographs from John Illingworth of Toronto, Canada, identifying himself as this *"unknown baby"*! He said it was an exciting moment for him to find in the book a picture almost identical to one in his possession (see below).

Bill Earle, Michael, Harry & Richard Rose and
(centre) young John Illingworth

Mr. Illingworth was born in Portsmouth in December 1938. During the war his father served in the Royal Navy, and John and his mother were evacuated to Fiddleford. Another lady with a baby daughter shared the same accommodation, and he remembers a wooden building, partitioned in the middle by a curtain to provide living spaces for the two mothers and babies. He says

"My mother (Gladys Illingworth) took a photo of these 'limited quarters' to send overseas to my Dad." This photograph is reproduced below — the inscription on the back of the original reads: *"This is the residence of Mrs. Illingworth and son, somewhere in England, October 1941."*

Connie Guttridge, who lived at the Post Office during the war, remembers this temporary accommodation well. It was an old chicken house which her mother, Mrs. Ridout, had bought before the war to use for parties (there was a piano in it) and as an extra room when visitors came to stay. The hut was situated in a part of the Post Office garden which extended along the back of **Meadowsweet (where Mr. Vic Caines and his wife, Ethel, lived).**

The hut (complete with dividing curtain) was home for a while to Mrs. Guttridge, her husband Tom and son Roger when they came back to live in Fiddleford in 1951. She described the row of small windows, with bigger ones below, which ran the whole length of the building. The large ones opened by folding downwards. Before the hut was erected on Mrs. Ridout's land, more height was obtained by putting in extra timber at the bottom.

Mr.Illingworth also recalled an old railway carriage, part of which can be seen in the background of the photograph on Page 102. According to Connie Guttridge, this was on Harry Rose's land (The Old Farmhouse) and was used to store grain. Nearby were three sheds, all of which were destroyed by fire during the war. One contained some dogs, which perished in the blaze.

Mr. Illingworth, though only a small child when he lived at Fiddleford, says he has "so many memories — the little post office run by Mrs. Ridout; sitting for hours on the wall outside Meadowsweet watching the army motorcyclists rounding the curve on their way to Blandford Forum camp. Also, the walks down to what we called 'The Weir' to go fishing with John Caines — and visits to my other 'Aunt' [Mrs. Ted Caines] in May Cottage. I distinctly remember 'Ma Beaven', and your description of her at the top of Page 145 [W.E.T.G.] describes her to a 'T'!!

My parents' association with Fiddleford (as well as mine and my sister's) did not end with the end of the war. We had become particularly close with Ethel and Vic Caines (known always to us kids as Auntie Ethel and Uncle Vic) and visited them regularly after the war and, of course, always stayed with them at Meadowsweet. You can imagine the emotions I experienced when I saw the pictures of Ethel and Vic (and Meadowsweet) in your book.

I emigrated to Canada in 1961 and I lost my Mother in 1972 and my Dad died in 1983 . . . . . "

[Footnote — Ethel Caines died in November 1991. She had been a widow for some years]

Standing — Jennie Ridout (left) and her daughter Rosa
Seated — Harriet Ridout with young John Illingworth

Harriet Ridout on her 80th birthday, with her sons Jack (left) and Jim

105

Kathleen Crew supplied the family chart reproduced below:

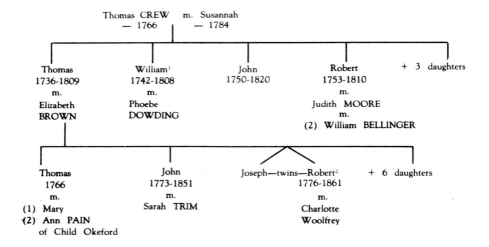

[1]   3 x great-grandparents of Cecil Crew (son of Renaldo and Lucy, nee Rose)
[2]   3 x great-grandparents of Brian Crew

POND VIEW

Mrs. Kathleen Crew has been researching her husband's family line. She says that Cecil Crew, who lived at Pond View in the late 1960's and early 1970's, was the son of Renaldo and Lucy (nee Rose) Crew. He was the 3 x great-grandson of William and Phoebe Crew of Stalbridge. Charles Crew, who was recorded in the 1839 Tithe Apportionment as tenant of pastureland at Pond Close, could have been Charles Crew 1805 - 1884, farmer of Cooks Farm, Stalbridge, who was Cecil's great-grandfather.

If this relationship is correct, it seems a great coincidence that a new bungalow should be built by the Pitt-Rivers estate at Pond Close (the name of the field) in the early 1950's, and that Cecil should become the tenant more than a hundred years after his ancestor had farmed there.

Mrs. Crew says that Dick, Kathleen Rhoda and Peter Raymond who were admitted to school in 1924, 1927 and 1933 respectively (W.E.T.G. Page 294/295) "were the children of Cornelius and Ella Crew. Cornelius was a fishmonger who, I am told, later went to Blandford. He was an uncle to Cecil Crew.

Flora Crew (1873-1915) married Harry Rose of The Old Farmhouse, Fiddleford. She was the daughter of Albert and Ellen Crew of Sturminster Newton, and sister of Renaldo and Cornelius. (W.E.T.G. Page 134)

Sam Rose, who lived at what is now called Knollbank, Fiddleford, (W.E.T.G. Page 106) married Bessie Beatrice Crew of Buckhorn Weston. I haven't yet been able to link Bessie's family with ours."

Robert Crew, blacksmith, in 1793 held "*Meadow Ground situate in a certain common mead called Fiddleford Mead (3A, 3R, 5P) and also that other piece of meadow ground situate in a certain place called Sudenham in a certain other common mead called Sedge Mead (o.1.33), for the lives of John Shrimpton, 70, butcher, the said Robert Crew 39 and Joseph Crew 16 son of Thomas Crew brother of said Robert Crew*"
[D.C.R.O. D.PIT/M65]

In October 1796, on surrendering two preceding leases, a new agreement for Pond Close in respect of Robert Crew was drawn up for the lives of Ann the wife of James King (weaver) 49, Robert Crew 43 and Judith his wife 24.

Kathleen Crew says "The son of Thomas and Susannah Crew of Stalbridge, he [Robert] became a blacksmith at Okeford Fitzpaine with his brother Thomas. Joseph, age 16, nephew of Robert, is mentioned on Page 102 of Where Elm Trees Grew — I have no other reference to him apart from his baptism. In his will Robert left everything to his wife Judith (land at Fiddlemead, Netherway Orchard lately purchased from James Butler, Pond Close and land unnamed at Okeford Fitzpaine and Belchalwell) and on her decease to his nephew Robert, Joseph's twin brother. Judith remarried — William Bellinger. I don't know if Robert did inherit. William Bellinger is mentioned on Page 88 in connection with land previously associated with Robert Snr."

Nephew Robert did inherit at least part of the above, as one of the following entries in the Sturminster Newton Court Book shows.

In the records of the villages of the Blackmore Vale the name Crew or Crewe occurs on numerous occasions, and it is difficult to fit all these into, or eliminate them from, this particular family line. Such a case is Ann Crew who on 5 April 1750 *"surrendered the lease for 'Scots Coppice adjacent to Piddleswood (5 acres)'* and Scot's Ground (2 acres of Meadow or Pasture) *'lying at Broad Oke adjacent to the said Wood or Coppice'."* [D.C.R.O. D.PIT/M.60]

At the Court Baron . . . . 30 October 1783 [Okeford Fitzpaine Court Book No. 4, Page 51] Robert Crew, blacksmith was granted *"one dwellinghouse, curtilage, garden and orchard containing three quarters of an acre"* for the lives of *"the said Robert Crew (about 31 years old) and Elizabeth Crew his wife (about 40 years old) for the term of their lives and the life of Robert Crew his nephew son of Thomas Crew blacksmith (about 7 years old)."* The rent was 1/6d [7½p] per year, heriot 5/- [25p], fine £35. [D.C.R.O. D.PIT/M62]

At the same Court on 17 October 1811 a Minute was noted that *"Robert Crew one of the Copyhold Tenants of this Manor died since the last Court possessed of a Copyhold Tenement by virtue of a Copy of Court Roll bearing date the Twenty Eighth day of November One Thousand Seven Hundred and Eightythree and that Judith Crew his Widow is the Lord's next Tenant for her Widowhood."* [D.C.R.O. D.PIT/M.63]

Judith Crew went to the Court *"and was admitted Tenant for her Widowhood and did to the said Lord her Fealty"* ['to do fealty' was the acknowledgement by a feudal tenant of fidelity to the lord]

'Copyhold Tenure' was the lease of property and land at the lord's decree, the 'Copy' being the transcript of the manorial court-roll containing a list of those tenants granted leases. A Copyholder normally enjoyed a certain security of tenure, since his tenancy agreement with the lord of the manor usually covered his lifetime and perhaps that of one or two other members of his family. More likely to lose his home was a labourer whose cottage was tied to his job. The requirements of the farmer for whom he worked (and perhaps this farmer was himself a tenant) might vary; circumstances necessitating a reduction in the number of men employed could result in the termination of the right to occupy a 'tied cottage'.

At the Court Baron on 12 October 1819 Robert Crew's nephew took over the tenancy, because *"Judith Crew Widow of Robert Crew late one of the Copyhold Tenants of this Manor hath intermarried with William Belringer whereby she hath forfeited her Widowhood Estate in the Dwellinghouse and Premises of which the said Robert Crew died possessed and that Robert Crew his Nephew is the next life named in the Copy of Court Roll . . . . . and the Lords next Tenant."* [D.C.R.O. D.PIT/M.63]

On the 17 October 1821 a Minute states *"To this Court came Robert Crew of Ockford Fitz-pain aforesaid Smith Son of Thomas Crew and Nephew of Robert Crew deceased and claimed to be admitted Tenant for his life to all that Messuage or Dwellinghouse Garden and Orchard containing by Admeasurement one Acre and Nine perches or thereabouts situate within this Manor of which the said Robert Crew his Uncle lately died possessed . . . . . "* Robert Crew, then aged *"Forty Five Years or thereabouts"* was admitted Tenant *"for his life at the Will of the Lord according to the custom of the said Manor by the Rent therefore by the Year of one Shilling and Six Pence and Five Shillings for an Heriot when it shall happen."*

Unfortunately the Court Books rarely give the location of cottages. Although the Robert Crew, blacksmith, mentioned at the Court in 1783 is obviously the same man as the Robert Crew who was 'a life' in the 1796 lease for Pond Close, Fiddleford, the property referred to in 1783 may or may not have been in Fiddleford — it is possible it was in the village of Okeford Fitzpaine.

In the Okeford Fitzpaine Tithe Apportionment, 1839, William Bellinger rented a half-acre in Sedge Mead and 3½ acres of meadow in Fiddleford Mead — both Meads mentioned in the 1793 Lease to Robert Crew. Presumably he was the *"William Belringer"* referred to in the Court Minute on 12 October 1819, being Judith Crew's second husband.

KNOLLBANK

MEMORIES OF THE LATE ELLEN (NELL) WAY, nee ROSE

One of seven sons, Sam Rose was born at Broad Oak. He later moved to Fiddleford, and he, his wife and nine children lived at Knollbank when it was a tiny thatched cottage.

One of his daughters, the late Mrs. Way of Child Okeford, talked in August 1988 about her childhood at Fiddleford. Sam would start work between 4.30 and 5 a.m., and one of her duties before going to school was to take his breakfast, hot eggs and bacon between two plates, from their home at Knollbank to Banbury — quite a walk.

She recalled Jo Cressey's pony — a white one, and that in addition to tools etc. he sold eggs. Mr. Savory, who lived at Willow Tree Cottage, made spars.

Because she was registered as a 'sweet manufacturer' during the 1939-1945 war, Miss Beaven was entitled to extra rations of sugar. She lived at Buff Cottage (now called Bryanston), where she made coconut ice, peppermint creams, hard-boiled and other sweets which she carried around in a wooden box on her old bicycle to sell in the nearby villages. She was an eccentric, well-known lady, still remembered by virtually everyone who lived in the area at that time. She was 88 years old when she died.

Mrs. Furnell, whose shop was at Snowdrop Cottage, used to make jam which was stored in large jars. She would then weigh it out in quantities of 1 lb. to be taken away by customers who brought their own containers.

Across the road, opposite Snowdrop Cottage, was a garden strip which belonged to Buff Cottage (Bryanston).

Mr. Rowland (who ran the slaughterhouse) had six German P.O.W.'s working for him during the war. They slept at Sturminster Union, and after they had finished work for the day the village boys 'escorted' them back there.

111

Some of the village children used to sit on stools near the fire —
which, said Mrs. Way, *"you could walk right round"* — at Mr. and
Mrs. Bill Goddard's house (part of Sweetwell).

Mrs. Way remembered that Mr. Joyce's predecessor as
gamekeeper was Mr. Gale, who had a daughter Lorna. Mr. Gale
lived at the cottage in Piddles Wood for several years before
moving to Hammoon.

Keeper's House, Piddles Wood

Sam Rose's uncle, John Rose, lived in one of the cottages at the
Mill — others were occupied by families called Tuck and Francis.
The house which is now The Paddock was a farm cottage for
Harry Rose's workers, and was occupied in succession by families
named Horlock, Elsworth and Jenkins.

Mrs. Way had many happy memories of Fiddleford and the close
community which was a natural result of the segregated situation
and small size of the hamlet. She died in 1991.

LITTLE BROOK

A HAPPY CHILDHOOD AT FIDDLEFORD

Dorothy (Dot) Byrne (nee Corbin), who now lives in Manchester, has put in writing her memories of Fiddleford. She has also supplied, in addition to splendid photographs of Granny Corbin and other members of her family, two pictures of the old Chapel (one exterior and one interior), which was something of a surprise since, when Where Elm Trees Grew was published, it appeared that no such photographs existed. Mrs. Byrne says "I don't know if all this will be of any interest, but I have enjoyed writing it and recalling my very happy childhood in a beautiful part of Dorset."

Here, in her own words, are her reminiscences.

"My mother (Kate Corbin, nee Caines) was born in the Travellers' Rest and her father — Thomas Caines — used to have a pony and trap and 'taxi' people to and from the railway station. [Thomas Caines died in 1908, aged 50.] My mother left school at fourteen and went into domestic service. She joined Ellen (Nellie), an older sister, in a house in Parkstone. She moved to various places and, with Nell as cook and mother as parlour-maid, they lived in Hampton Court Palace for several years, and she used to tell us stories about boating on the Thames with the soldiers from the nearby barracks.

When Granny Caines became ill, mother came home for a while, then took several jobs in local big houses, so that she could be with her mother more often. At the time of her marriage to my father in 1923 she was cook at Long Lynch House in Shillingstone for a family called Knights — part of the Knights soap manufacturers.

My parents met when he was home on leave from France (1914-18 war) and he was staying with his mother, who lived in the house near the railway in Scots Ground. Mother was at home looking after her mother, and was shaking a mat outside when father walked down Front Lane and that was it. They both came

113

Emily Kate Corbin (nee Caines) when in service

from Fiddleford, but as they were both away, hadn't really met before.

They lived in Broad Oak for a while — Fred and I were born there — but when Uncle Ted moved to May Cottage after Granny Caines died, we moved to Fiddleford (I was two).

Maria (Granny) Caines (1858-1928), mother of Emily Kate

Granny Caines

When mother went away, she sent her first earnings to her mother — £3 a quarter (three months), and on her first visit home, brought her a cream jug and sugar basin. The basin has been broken for many years, but I have the jug on my 'Dorset' shelf with some ornaments that belonged to Granny Caines, as well as some from my mother's home.

GLOVE-MAKING

My mother used to make these kid gloves and used a treadle machine we called a donkey. The material was held in a vice-like contraption — each side had 10-12 teeth. The needle was passed to and fro through the openings, thus ensuring the stitches were even. (The treadle was only for operating the opening and closing of the jaws I think.)

MAY COTTAGE

This was where the family gathered for tea on Christmas Day (the Caines — Ted and Vic — and Corbins). There was a huge tree in the living room with real candles that clipped on the branches — highly dangerous — and lots of presents under the tree. The table was full of food and fruit, jelly and cakes and of course crackers. Later we played games and had the run of the house. Jack used to organise a treasure hunt and one year we were all upstairs looking for clues when there was an ominous crack — one of the floor boards had given a bit. We were all called down and I think we sat around waiting for the house to fall down! [Jack and Topsy were the children of Ted and Lou Caines.]

Topsy used to play the piano for a sing-song, and we always ended up by everyone sitting round the table playing 'Tip-it'.

Uncle Ted used to keep a couple of cows — sometimes in the orchard or sometimes over a wooden bridge into the field opposite the house. This has now become part of the large field. At hay-making time they borrowed a horse and cart from Rose's at the Mill and everyone would lend a hand. We children were

117

Mrs. Harry Corbin (nee Emily Kate Caines)

allowed to ride in the cart when it was empty and we loved bumping across the field. When all the hay had been gathered, there was a huge picnic tea for everyone in the field.

One year when the horse was crossing this bridge, one of his legs went through the wood — the poor thing was firmly stuck and it took ages to free him. It delayed getting the hay in but we children loved all the excitement. [The bridge was demolished some years ago, as it had become unsafe.]

May Cottage was the place

(1) where we first heard the radio. Aunt Lou had a set before we did, and Fred and I used to go there on Mondays and listen to 'Monday Night at Eight'.

(2) where you could always get lovely plums and apples.

(3) where you couldn't get to when the flood waters were high. Topsy and Jack had to clamber over the garden hedge on to Back Lane, with their bikes, to go to school.

(4) where my husband Terry stayed the night before our wedding in 1947.

(5) where the eldest member of the family lived, and we all gathered there when our Canadian cousin came to Fiddleford on leave for the first time early in the 1939-45 war. He was the son of my mother's sister Mabel — she emigrated to Canada on a one-way ticket as a domestic servant in 1912, three weeks after the Titanic was sunk. She came back forty-five years later and expected everything to be as it was when she left — some things hadn't altered much actually. Of course, she too stayed at May Cottage.

She was two years older than my mother, born at the Travellers' Rest, left school at fourteen to go into domestic work, and then decided to go to Canada when she was eighteen. She had to undertake to stay with the same family for at least two years. In fact, she probably stayed with them until her marriage to a local policeman.

119

Lou and Ted Caines, with Ted's sister Mabel (from Canada)
taken in Front Lane under the may tree outside May Cottage
(probably mid 1960's)

They had three children — all now retired. Evelyn, the eldest
daughter, was an Art Teacher and her husband a Headmaster of a
College. They had three boys, and now have several grandchildren.
Evelyn and Tom [her husband] have been to England several times,
staying at Fiddleford, with Jack and Milly [Caines] and with us here
in Manchester.

The two boys, Ken and George (both married), came to England
and Europe with the Canadian Army in the 1939-45 war. Ken
worked in Insurance and George followed his father into the
Police Force and was a Royal Mountie for many years.

Mabel died in 1984, aged 90 or so.

May Cottage for me holds many happy memories — family
meetings and parties, picnics, lovely flowers, may trees in bloom,

Canadian cousin Ken's first visit to 'May Cottage', 1942
l. to r. Ted Caines, Lou Caines, Ken, Kate Corbin and Walter Theophilus,
son of Alf Caines (Lou Caines's brother) from Blandford

Jack's smelly maggots — he used to 'breed' his own at the very
top of the garden, Uncle Ted's sheds, the lovely smells in the
kitchen after a baking session, the variety of birds that Aunt Lou
seemed to be able to attract to the bird table and the beautiful
kingfisher whose favourite haunt was on a willow tree near the
corner of the front paddock.

[In later years, 1970-1989, various kingfishers spent long periods — 20 or 30 minutes
sometimes — on a dead branch we had positioned over the pool in the front garden. It
was a fairly common occurrence, and watching them gave us so much pleasure. O.A.H.]

KNOLL BANK

Sam Rose of Knoll Bank was a character. He had a huge picture
of 'The Relief of Ladysmith' — it practically covered the whole
wall. He used to tell us about the Middle East (General Gordon
riding in on his horse etc.) and the Boer War — of course, Sam
was there. His pride and joy was an old battered half lb. tin which

121

had once been full of chocolates. On the occasion of Queen Victoria's Diamond Jubilee every serving soldier was given a souvenir tin. This was silver-coloured with an enamelled picture of the Queen on the lid. The tin was full of dust, but to Sam it was very precious and we were only allowed to look — not touch.

He had a great liking for the eels we used to catch in the brook. We put in baited hooks tied to string, or fishing line if we could afford it, leave overnight, and we very often had an eel on the end in the morning.

The stream, years ago, was very well maintained. Everyone would keep their bit of it clean, weeds cut back and trees trimmed. My father tethered his goats in the lane sometimes, and Uncle Ted used to let his cows there (under supervision) to keep the grass down. The water was used for the gardens etc. before the pipes were laid for a regular supply.

After Mr. and Mrs. Eaton left, a Mr. and Mrs. Kirkland lived there for several years. I think he was retired, but Mrs. Kirkland was a teacher working at Croft House School in Shillingstone.

After they left, the house was modernised and a young couple moved into it — John and Ruth Everett. John worked on the land I think. The couple later moved to a farm in Devon.

CAMELBACK COTTAGE (Littlebrook)

My mother's brothers, who were in the Army, would address the envelopes to Camelback Cottage when writing to their mother (pre 1914-18 war).

When Ted Caines lived there, it was virtually three houses — each having its own stairs and back and front doors. Ted lived in the left hand third, Granny Caines lived in the centre and, as it was a 'mill cottage', a worker from the mill lived in the other part.

When Granny Caines became ill she was looked after by Aunt Lou [Mrs. Ted Caines] so the two houses really became one, and remained so when we moved into it. (It was great having two sets of stairs when playing hide and seek!)

I think Percy Gregory was probably living in the other part then — he was the miller at that time but I don't know anything about him. I can see him yet though — covered in dust and his eyebrows and moustache thick with the white dust from milling the corn.

Littlebrook, or No. 3, was altered inside considerably by Rivers Estate in the late '30's or early 40's. The back kitchen and bedroom were taken from Granny Caines' part and added to the smaller part, making it into two houses.

After Gregorys went to live at Shillingstone, Fred Yeatman moved in. Later Jim Goddard and his wife Ivy lived there with their son Norman. Jim was a son of Hetty Goddard of Sweetwell, and Ivy was the daughter of Bill Eaton who lived in the railway cottage. Later Ivy's brother Harold Eaton and his wife Dora lived there for a time.

l. to r. Fred Corbin with his two sons, Bryan & Phillip; his sister Dot & her son Tony; & Mrs. Harry Corbin with her grandson (Dot's son) Terence
August, 1958

123

The last family living there was Morris and Margaret Ridout —
Morris was Jack Ridout's son from Woodlands Farm. (This is the
right spelling of his name — Morris was his mother Annie's
maiden name.) The house stood empty for many years after that.

SWEETWELL

When Goddards lived there, there were two houses. A Miss Pike
lived in the smaller one. I can't remember much about her except
that to us she was very old and had great difficulty in getting
about. After she died, the house remained empty.

There was an old cockerel that used to live at the Mill. He was
far better than any watch-dog and would attack anybody and
anything. We always hoped that he'd be busy when we went past.
Mrs. Goddard used to go across the fields regularly to
Sturminster, and had a handy stick at each end of the Mill so that
she could defend herself — which she had to do very often.

My mother used to help at the Mill House and she would arm
herself with a stick from the wood-pile before going in. Very
often she'd come home and tell us that the cockerel had *"had a
good wop today"*. She always said that it was so tough no-one
would ever be able to eat it. I can't remember how he met his
end, but we were very relieved to know he had gone — he was a
horror.

MANOR FARM HOUSE

After the Elkins family left, the house was modernised and a Mr.
and Mrs. Torrance Scott lived there. Mr. Scott was a retired Shell
Executive and had been a diplomat in Switzerland. Unfortunately
he died within a few years (November 1960), but Mrs. Scott
continued to live there on her own until the early 1970's, when
she moved to Worthing. She died there in October 1989.

The barn she called The Dairy, and used it for storing vegetables
etc. — it was a separate building then.

WILLOW TREE COTTAGE

This cottage always reminds me of Sundays. Granny Corbin was my father's mother, and after Chapel on Sunday evenings we always called in to see her. To us she was very strict and we had to be seen and not heard. Eric Fudge (my cousin) joined the R.A.F. before the war, and I can't remember him living with Granny, but he stayed with her when he came home on leave.

ARCHWAY HOUSE

A Mr. and Mrs. Thomas lived in the house (1940-ish) when he retired from being Master at the old Workhouse in Sturminster. His sister-in-law, Miss Brooks, lived in the adjoining cottage [now part of the Inn] between Woodview and Archway. They were there for several years, but I have no dates (I think they were there — probably not Mrs. Thomas — when I left Fiddleford in 1947).

My mother used to help Charlie Adams on Saturday mornings. He was very interested in metalwork — particularly brasswork, and mother would clean and polish the items for him. When she was eight, he made a tray for her as a present, and I have it now, so that is nearly ninety years old.

SNOWDROP COTTAGE

My mother talked of going to the shop at Mrs. Furnell's. In the 1930's my father had an offer to purchase Snowdrop for £50. That was a lot of money then and he turned the offer down, much to the annoyance of my mother who would have liked to have opened a little tea-shop there.

KEEPER'S COTTAGE

I was very friendly with Vera Dymond and often used to visit the house. I can confirm that there were some stone walls in the rooms at the back of the house, and it always seemed very cold there. As far as I know there was never any electricity to the house, and they used paraffin for cooking and lighting, and batteries for the radio. Accumulators for the radio were re-charged at Percy Rose's Garage at The Bridge — we all used these accumulators for our radios then of course.

Mr. Dymond used to raise hundreds of partridge and pheasant chicks for Captain Pitt-Rivers, who owned all the land around. Every winter they held big shooting sessions for these birds and rabbits and hares — the biggest shoot was always held on Boxing Day.

THE CHAPEL

The photograph of Harvest Time in the Chapel must have been taken prior to 1930 or so, as I can only remember the pulpit being on the left hand side of the picture, in the corner, and the organ was to the right hand side.

The decorating was similar most years — Mrs. Elkins from Manor Farm House always did the pulpit. I can remember re-covering the 'Harvest Home' letters several times with red or green crepe paper.

The coconut matting is just about visible, and this ran the length of the Chapel. There were coat hooks on the walls above the pews, and more hooks in the entrance. The only time I can remember the Chapel being really packed was at Harvest and Anniversary time.

THE METHODIST CHURCH

This Long Service Certificate

is presented to

H. L. Corbin

who was received as a fully accredited Local Preacher in the year 1930 and in this capacity has continued to render loyal and devoted service to the Church of Christ and the Kingdom of God June 1970.

President of the Conference

Local Preachers' Department

L†P

Mrs. Byrne's father, Harry Corbin, was a Local Preacher, and a steadfast worker at Fiddleford Chapel

THE RAILWAY COTTAGE

Elizabeth (Granny) Corbin and family lived in the railway cottage for many years. Her husband James was a 'ganger' on the railway and a condition of living in the house was that they acted as crossing keepers. James died in April 1913, aged 77.

Granny Corbin with her three youngest daughters —
Jess, Ivy and (seated) Lily

Harry Corbin was born in the Railway Cottage in 1891 — the address given when the birth was registered was *"Hammoon Crossing"*. There were eight other children in the family — Ethel, Arthur, May, Jessie, Tom, Ivy, Lily and another child who died in infancy. Apart from the fact that my father went to school in Okeford Fitzpaine, we don't know much about their life — most of the children moved away when they left school.

It all sounds idyllic, and in a way I suppose it was. But everyone was, by today's standards, very poor, though well fed. When my parents left the tied cottage, Littlebrook, in 1970, they were paying 8/- [40p] per week rent to the Mill. Father retired at seventy (receiving no pension during the time he was working). On his retirement he was paid £6 per year — 2/6d [12½p] per week — in addition to the state pension. The supplement was 6d [2½p] per week for each year worked after the age of 65. I don't know how much the basic pension was then.

My mother worked at the Mill, cleaning and washing (no washing machine then) for 6d per hour.

Nevertheless it was a happy community. During the summer holidays the children spent much of the time down by the river, swimming and fishing.

The children who went to Blandford Grammar School had to cycle to Shillingstone Station and get the train. We didn't often miss it, but a lot of times it was only because the guard had seen us tearing down the road and would do a 'go slow' for us. We would just throw our bikes in the hedge and know they would still be there when we returned (a sign of the times!). There was a lovely old guard who was on regularly — a big man with lovely rosy cheeks, lots of white hair and a huge white moustache which nearly covered his face. He always wore a flower in his buttonhole, and in the spring we used to take him some of the first primroses — perhaps that helped a bit!

One time there was a goat tethered at Blandford Station for several days. I mentioned it to my father and he said he'd ordered

130

Granny Corbin with her two eldest grandsons —
Harold Corbin (son of Granny's eldest son, Arthur, who lived in Portsmouth
and was in the Royal Navy pre-1914) and (right) Eric Fudge

131

a goat from a firm in Lincolnshire but had heard nothing more about it. On checking at the Station, it was decided that this was the goat, but the railway authorities didn't know where to deliver it as the goat had eaten its label. Father had to walk it home from Shillingstone Station, but it was none the worse for that as we had her for many years and she was the best milker we'd ever had.

After we stopped keeping the goats we had to fetch our milk from Jack Ridout's at Woodlands Farm — he was the only farmer in Fiddleford who sold milk. We'd take our one pint cans to the farm and Mrs. Ridout would fill them from a huge churn, ladling the milk out with a long-handled measure. It's a good job the cans had lids or we would have spilled half of the milk before we got home.

When pasteurisation of milk became compulsory all small outlets like this were banned, so milk was then delivered in bottles from Sturminster Newton.

Nothing was ever wasted — spare fruit and vegetables were either stewed, pickled or salted or made into jams and chutney. We picked wild fruits like sloes, elderberries, blackberries and dandelions to make wines and spare eggs were put in waterglass to be used when the hens were having a 'rest'. We gathered chestnuts from Piddleswood, put them in an airtight tin with some salt and buried them in the garden — to be retrieved and eaten at Christmas time.

Bonfire night was a community affair. We had a huge bonfire in the field at the top of Front Lane. Percy Rose at the Garage saved his old tyres for us, and we had flames leaping up so high they would scorch the leaves on the old elm trees. Fireworks were shared, and we made lanterns from hollowed out turnips and stuck candles inside. Fireworks lasted much longer in those days. One year, the local policeman was there, and the big lads pinned a double rip-rap on his jacket. It took him ages trying to get it off — much to the amusement of all!! He wasn't very popular actually, as he used to lie in wait and try and catch us when we didn't have lights on our bikes — he wasn't very successful at that either!!

When we were old enough for school, most of the Fiddleford children went to the Junior School in Sturminster (now William Barnes School) — we had to walk the two miles as there were no buses then.

When it was dry enough we walked across the fields from Fiddleford Mill — much quicker than the roads. There was a big hollow tree in the hedge at the end of the field called Little Ham and we used to love to climb up inside it and look out of a hole about six feet up in the trunk.

Occasionally walking home via the road we'd meet up with Fred Yeatman, on his way back to the mill after delivering the corn and meal to the farmers. He hardly ever gave us a lift but we used to hang on to the back of the cart and get pulled along.

Travelling around in the 30's and 40's was difficult and a bike was essential. At this time there were only two cars in Fiddleford — one belonged to Rupert Rose and the other to Mr. Thomas. There were no tractors and the only power was horse — the four-legged kind.

You could travel further afield of course — by train from Sturminster or Shillingstone stations or on the Royal Blue bus which passed through Fiddleford. The Royal Blue Company operated long distance coaches that travelled from Cheltenham to Bournemouth every day (one each way — twice a day). You had to 'book' a seat, giving three days' notice, and then the coach would stop and pick you up. There were two local 'booking offices' — one was at the Red Lion at Newton and the other was Rose's, the printers in Bridge Street, Sturminster.

From Cheltenham buses travelled to all parts of the country. The trains went to Bournemouth or to Templecombe, which then was a very busy station with huge sidings so that the trains could be shunted on to different tracks to continue to Bath or London. At this time the trains were so regular and on time that locals could

tell the time by them — e.g. The Pines Express to Bournemouth
— 4.30 p.m. — time to go home for tea!

SUNDAY SCHOOL OUTINGS

The only time we saw the sea was on the annual Sunday School
outings from the Bridge Methodist Church, which were arranged
by the Superintendent, Jabez Cluett. He was a saddler and kept a
leather shop in Bridge St., opposite the entrance to the
Recreation Ground. He arranged for several coaches (charabancs)
to take the parents and children to either Weymouth or Swanage
— Weymouth was the most popular.

The coaches at that time were individually owned by garage
proprietors (Knight's of Hazelbury Bryan and Sales of Sturminster
were two).

Dot Corbin, her brother Fred and her cousins at a Sunday School outing at
Weymouth, June 1934

(back row) Jack Caines, Harry Fudge
(left) Topsy Caines (middle row) Fred Corbin, Sid Fudge
(front row) Ida Caines, John Caines, Dot Corbin

There was great excitement as we set off armed with sandwiches, buckets and spades etc. and 'pennies for Woolworth's'. It was a huge treat for us to be able to go into a big shop with such an array of goodies for 3d or 6d [2½p].

When we got past Dorchester we had special things to look out for — the hillside where the train suddenly disappeared into the tunnel, the gap in the hills where you could see the sea on the horizon and then the big U bend at Upwey that meant you were nearly there. Then the prom and the swans on Radipole Lake near where the coaches parked.

We usually went shopping in the morning and then went to the Nothe to hunt for crabs and shrimps in the rock pools. As we walked back there was always a sand artist on the beach who built marvellous sand models of cathedrals and churches. At 5 p.m. or 5.30 p.m. we all met under the clock on the front to go to Tett's restaurant for 'high tea'.

It must have been an awful din on the way home — most of us had bought gazoos or bugles, and, if not, a comb with some tissue paper over it and a good blow would make quite a passable noise!

It was a wonderful day out and we all thoroughly enjoyed it.

The first time my husband's parents came to Fiddleford from Manchester they were fascinated by the oil lamps, candles and cooking facilities (there was no electricity in the village until 1958 so there was no choice). The one thing that [Terry's] Dad couldn't get over was meeting Uncle Ted's cows at close quarters in the front lane!

My parents celebrated their Golden Wedding on the 6th June 1973 and we arranged a surprise party for them in the Sturminster Hall. When they arrived they were welcomed by a 'choir' of friends and relatives singing 'Here Comes The Bride'. Don't know what they were most surprised about — the party or the singing!!

Our youngest son, Tony, loved Fiddleford and used to wander all over the place. Grandpop's sheds were a delight to him, and he still has several tools that he 'acquired' then.

Family gathering at Sturminster Hall on the occasion of Kate and Harry Corbin's Golden Wedding, 6th June 1973

My daughter Janet and Tony used to love to go into Rose's farm (Sweetwell) when they were milking, and Richard [Rose] used to sit Janet on the Jersey cow's back.

Mrs. Mitchell, who lived in The Paddock, had a pet sheep called Basil, and Mrs. Rose at the Mill had two pet sheep, Gert and Daisy, and in the Spring Janet was allowed to feed the lambs with a bottle. They had lovely holidays there — a pity it all had to end."

* * * * * * * * * *

[This is the end of the contribution from Dorothy Byrne]

Dorothy Byrne's brother, Fred Corbin, also wrote with additional information about Sweetwell.

He says "Mrs. Hetty Goddard (with sons Percy and Harry) occupied the southernmost of the two cottages and Miss Pike the other side, until they moved to council houses in Rixon, Sturminster Newton in the middle 1930's.

The two cottages were then extensively refurbished and converted into one dwelling by the Rivers Estate workforce, and it was then occupied by Mr. Charles Galpin and his wife. He was the architect for the Rivers Estate, and during the war he acted as the Rural District Council A.R.P. Controller, as well as running the local Air Training Corps.

The house was later occupied by Mr. Conway who was, I believe, farm manager for the Estate. He later took over some land at Bulbarrow and farmed it on his own account, until he was killed in a farm accident up there. His widow (who was Scottish) married Mr. Albrecht the chemist from Sturminster Newton and he came to live in the house after the marriage."

WOODVIEW

Silas Cressey lived at Woodview for almost fifty years in the second half of the 19th century [W.E.T.G. Page 123/4]. His wife and children worked in the family business, making leather goods.

In the 1861 Census returns, Silas himself is described as *"fellmonger and hosier"*. A fellmonger was a worker in leather. His wife Rachel was a *"gater maker (corse leather)"* [sic]; the eldest son was a *"fellmonger and glovecutter"*; Edith, aged 14, a *"gater maker"* and Joseph, 10, a *"skinner"*.

He, or one of his sons, eventually (probably c.1895) obtained premises in Sturminster Newton. It was common to have small articles to give to customers, as firms sometimes now distribute pencils etc. as an advertising medium. On the opposite page is a photograph of one of the blotters given away by S. Cressey & Son. They were about 6 x 4 inches [15 cm x 10 cm approximately]. On the underside was thick pink blotting paper (no ball-point pens in those days!) and on the upper side were pictures, most of which were of the 'chocolate-box' type. One however was different, and showed ingenuity. It was a play on the family name, and depicted the Black Prince, pierced with arrows, after the Battle of Crecy [Cressy] in 1346, with the caption:

"The Black Prince After Cressy" — "English History Humorously Illustrated"

"It was here the Black Prince too commenced to evince
His good claim to renown, which he's kept ever since."

The date of the blotter is unknown, but from the fact that it gives a telephone number (No. 16), it was probably 1920/1930 or maybe even later.

Mrs. Evelyn Maude Fellowes Andrews of Ealing lived at Woodview for about six years (from approximately 1906-1912). She was then Maude Fry. Here are her reminiscences of those early days at Fiddleford, in her own words:

139

"My father was Manager of Blandford & Webb's — Corn, Seed and Coal Merchants at Sturminster. We first lived at Newton, where I was born. The family consisted of one boy, then five girls.

I don't know when we moved to Fiddleford, but I think about 1906 — to Woodview — which was at that time red-brick — with a chapel either next door or in the garden! There was a well in the yard at the back.

I remember the Adams family who lived next door — at what is now Fiddleford Inn. I don't remember much about Nellie, but her brother Colin became an actor and we kept in touch for many years after we left Fiddleford. They had a beautiful Old English Sheepdog called Caesar — a great friend.

My brother went to the Boys' School at Sturminster; my eldest sister, Dot, went to Miss Bell's private school; Florrie and Win to the C. of E. School. They walked together across the fields. My youngest sister was born blind, so she went away to school at Southsea when she was six years old.

On Page 216 [Where Elm Trees Grew] you mention "a little scholar died on her way to school in Feb. 1908". That was my sister Florrie. On their way to school they used to pick some of the 'horse beans', and Florrie choked. A passer-by, I believe a school-teacher, brought her home dead. She was six years old. I was told that some of her little school friends carried her coffin. She is buried at Sturminster cemetery along with my father, my mother's ashes and my youngest sister's ashes. My brother's name is on the stone — he was killed in World War I in 1918 at nineteen years.

We moved to Sturminster in 1912, to a new house which had the reputation of being the first house in the area to have a purpose-built bathroom! This was The Laurels in Bath Road (formerly called White Lane). I was now six years old, so I started school. The girl sitting next to me was Mona Rose, and we became lifelong friends. She is pictured in Where Elm Trees Grew among the teachers — she is, or was, cousin to Rupert and Howard Rose at the Mill. I must just note here that we learnt our alphabet with

140

sand and slates — I can still remember doing the capitals with my fingers in the sand!

Miss L. Beale, who became Mrs. Clark, was the Junior Mistress and of course Maggie Rose was Head. She was very strict, but she was an excellent teacher and Head. I later went to Blandford Secondary School, but I always think I was lucky to start where I did.

My father was a Quaker — Fry. My mother was C. of E. So they compromised — we all went to the Wesleyan Chapel and to Sunday School where Mr. Wilkins was the Sunday School Superintendent. I still have the Bible given me by him in April 1916.

Mona and I often spent time at Fiddleford, as we loved swimming in the mill stream. We often picnicked there. One February day, when the fields were flooded and you could not see the river from the field, we walked straight into the river! Fortunately we could both swim. I got into fearful trouble for ruining my clothes — we didn't try that again.

I was very impressed with the Manor House [during a visit in 1988]. I remember seeing some sort of building near the Mill House, but just thought it was a farm building.

I remember Mrs. Furnell's sweet shop, and what a bad-tempered woman she was. As kids we used to stand outside and argue who was brave enough to go in and spend our half-penny!"

Mrs. Fellowes Andrews later explained that 'horse beans' were very similar to broad beans, the real difference being they were not staked but grown all over the fields like turnips or potatoes, and of course were horse fodder." [The Reader's Digest Encyclopaedic Dictionary describes a horse bean as "Variety of Vicia faba grown for fodder". Vicia faba is the species name for broad bean]

Bryanston, 1987

142

BRYANSTON

David Wright of Blandford published, in October 1990, a fascinating book called David and Joan. It is largely auto-biographical, but in addition to anecdotes from "here and around the world", as he puts it, there is a tremendous amount of interesting information regarding Blandford and the surrounding area.

One small episode concerns the cottage Mr. Wright bought in Fiddleford. He thinks it must have been in 1933 when he acquired it, in a condition which today would no doubt be described as 'suitable for improvement'.

In 1932 it was purchased by Dorset County Council, as they needed part of the garden for road-widening purposes. Having severed the strip of land they required, the Council then put on the market the remainder of the property (which included the house), for which estate agents Senior and Godwin asked £30. Mr. Wright offered £25, and eventually a compromise of £27.10s was agreed.

The new owner spent a week of his fortnight's annual holiday camping in a tent in the field opposite, befriended by Mrs. Ridout, and working on the cottage with a builder in the day time. In Mr. Wright's own words "it only required general repairs, a new concrete floor for the back lobby and concrete slabs raised on brick piers on the tops of the two chimneys to keep the rain out. The thatch at that time was quite good but I had to redecorate inside and out."

He goes on to explain that he went to buy some distemper for use on the outside, and buff was recommended as a suitable colour. Thus the name of the refurbished building presented no problem — he called it simply and logically Buff Cottage.

His first tenant, who paid 6/- [30p] per week, was a bank official. This amount was arrived at by deducting from a rent of 10/- [50p] a discount of 4/- until the expected arrival of mains water.

However, when this long-anticipated event materialised and tap-water was installed in the cottage, the bank official went elsewhere!

Miss Agnes Platt then lived there for a while. When she left, it was sold to Miss Ellen Beaven for £160. In addition to the original purchase price of £27.10s.0d, Mr. Wright had spent £80 on the house, plus a week's work carrying out the necessary repairs.

He now wonders when, why and by whom the cottage was re-named Bryanston.

AINGERS FARM

The following photographs were supplied by the Cross family (Victor, Hilda and Averil) who spent their childhood at Aingers Farm, and lived there until 1947.

Aingers Farm from the air, taken at 1000 ft. [approx 304.5 metres] at 200 m.p.h. July 1939

145

William Cross at Sturminster Newton Market, early 1920's.
Note the wooden pens

Hilda Cross, aged 3 and Victor Cross, aged 5 on Nigger the pony, which Hilda also rode. Nigger was used in a governess cart for transport. The roof of Aingers Farm House can be seen in the background

Victor Cross (aged 10) and Gip the dog seated on a boat waggon used mostly for haymaking. The photograph was taken in the orchard at Aingers Farm

From left to right — Hilda (12) and Averil (6) Cross and Joan Thomas (12) on pram wheels, used for rides down the hill at Lodge Farm. Averil says *"This was one of the ways in which we enjoyed ourselves. We had to make our own amusements — very different from the modern days."* Photograph — early 1930's

Averil Cross — Sports Day, Blandford Grammar School, 1938.
Averil is shown here with the cups she won for High Jump, Long Jump
and — a great achievement — Victor Ludorum

Hilda Cross, Mrs. Short and Mr. Vincent (signalman at Shillingstone Station)
potato-ing at Aingers Farm

Everyone was involved in the war effort from 1939-1945. The job of farmers and their families was to produce the maximum yield from their land.

During the war, Averil Cross was called up to report to A.T.S. Training Centre, Northampton. After training, she was sent to South Eastern Technical College, Dagenham, for a course on general office duties. She was then posted to A.T.S. Records Office, Winchester, where she remained until demobilisation. A.T.S. Records Office was a very large establishment where many civilians were also employed.

Averil Cross, 1943

Fred Trowbridge in the uniform of a telegraph boy

LODGE FARM

Mrs. Joan Goodwin (nee Thomas) has supplied four photographs taken at Lodge Farm (where she lived) before the Second World War.

Lodge Farm House c. 1927

151

Mr. Trowbridge farmed at Lodge Farm for thirty years. He was a native of
Fiddleford. Here he is haymaking with his sons Harry and Leslie

Blossom, ready for work, in the yard at Lodge Farm

During the last two of his forty-four years with the Post Office, where he started at the age of fourteen, Fred Trowbridge was supervisor at Sturminster Newton.

During the war he served with the 4th Dorsetshire Regiment and took part in the allied invasion of France. He died suddenly at the age of fifty-eight.

Mrs. Vera Upshall has supplied the names of the people in this photograph About to Hunt Rabbits, which appeared on Page 156 of Where Elm Trees Grew. They are, from left to right:

Frank Trowbridge (senior), Bert Trowbridge, Sidney Fox, Wilfred Rose, Tom Knott, Charlie Phillips (seated), Reuben Trowbridge (sailor), Hugh Fudge, Maurice Trowbridge, Fred Rose (sitting on gate), Fred Trowbridge, Charlie Upshall (sitting on gate)

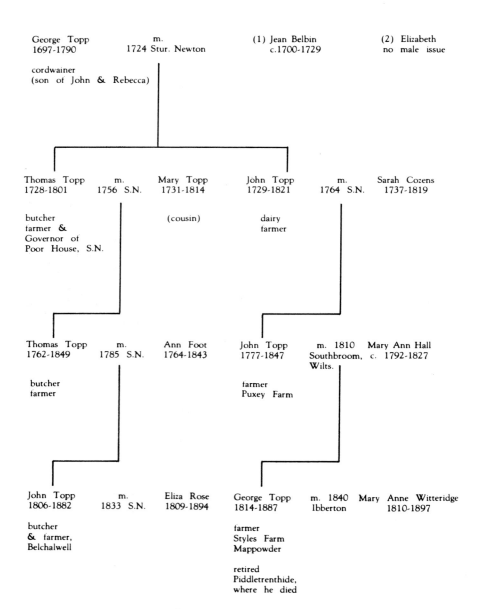

George Topp   m.   (1) Jean Belbin   (2) Elizabeth
1697-1790   1724 Stur. Newton   c.1700-1729   no male issue

cordwainer
(son of John & Rebecca)

Thomas Topp   m.   Mary Topp   John Topp   m.   Sarah Cozens
1728-1801   1756 S.N.   1731-1814   1729-1821   1764 S.N.   1737-1819

butcher   (cousin)   dairy
farmer &   farmer
Governor of
Poor House, S.N.

Thomas Topp   m.   Ann Foot   John Topp   m. 1810   Mary Ann Hall
1762-1849   1785 S.N.   1764-1843   1777-1847   Southbroom, c. 1792-1827
                                                                Wilts.
butcher   farmer
farmer   Puxey Farm

John Topp   m.   Eliza Rose   George Topp   m. 1840   Mary Anne Witteridge
1806-1882   1833 S.N.   1809-1894   1814-1887   Ibberton   1810-1897

butcher   farmer
& farmer,   Styles Farm
Belchalwell   Mappowder

                                               retired
                                               Piddletrenthide,
                                               where he died

WOODLANDS FARM

Charles Topp was a butcher who lived at Woodlands Farm, Fiddleford for some forty years or more (from about 1870 or maybe a little earlier). Very little was known about him and his family until Kenneth Topp, a great-nephew who lives in Yorkshire, sent photographs and more information. This chapter has been compiled from the results of his research.

Charles (1833-1911) was one of the seven sons of John Topp (1806-1882), master butcher, farmer and grazier, and his wife Eliza (1809-1894), who were married in 1833 at Sturminster Newton. Eliza was the daughter of Thomas and Ann Rose. From 1843 until their deaths John and Eliza lived at Knackershole Farm (now called Knoll Farm), Okeford Common. They are both buried under a tree in a very secluded corner of an extension at the far end of Fifehead Cemetery.

The sketch of their tombstone was done from a photograph taken by Kenneth Topp some twelve or more years ago. It shows Eliza's age as 81 at her death, but she was in fact 85 (born 14 April 1809; baptised 30 April 1809). Kenneth Topp wonders about the discrepancy — was it the result of a stonemason's error, did Eliza during her lifetime deliberately disguise her true age (a practice employed by ladies throughout the ages!), or had she been genuinely ignorant of the year of her birth?

Some 34 of the 40 acres of Knackershole Farm were sold in 1874 to George Broad, farmer, of Lower Fifehead.

Herbert Topp (1855-1928), younger brother of Charles, and sixth of the seven brothers, took over the house, stables, cowstalls, piggeries etc. in 1894 after the death of his mother. Herbert was a farmer and miller and had for some years occupied the Water Grist Mill and house with adjoining meadows near the Packhorse Bridge at Fifehead Neville. In 1917, after a fire caused by a thunderbolt, Herbert sold the house and land at Knackershole to Tom Rose Trowbridge of Okeford Fitzpaine, who restored and improved the house. In 1981 the property came on the market again — it was advertised by the agents as "Detached Character Farmhouse with fine country views. 4 bedrooms, 3 living rooms, extensive outbuildings, about 4 acres" and offers in the region of £60,000 were invited for the freehold. Herbert retired to live at Ferndown, Dorset and later moved to Blandford, where he died in 1928.

At Sherborne in September 1865 Charles Topp married Mary Ann Marphus (widow), daughter of Daniel Bright, a baker, and his first wife Mary (nee Jenkins). Mary Ann was baptised in 1830 at Sturminster Newton where, in September 1851, she married her first husband, John Robins Marphus. She was a handsome woman, as can be seen from the photograph. Charles and Mary Ann lived at Woodlands Farm, Fiddleford, where Charles pursued his trade from the farm, a circuit of inns in the locality, and Poole Quay (for the Newfoundland shipping).

FAMILY OF CHARLES TOPP OF WOODLANDS FARM

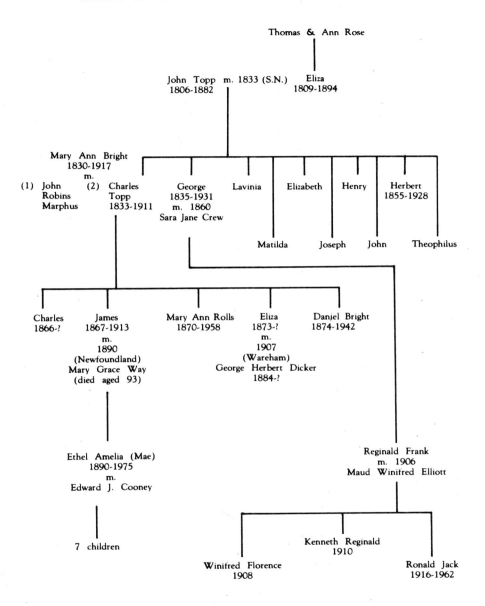

KNACKERSHOLE (KNOLL FARM), OKEFORD COMMON, near STURMINSTER NEWTON,
DORSET (circa 1860)

Charles and Mary Ann had five children — three boys and two girls, all of whom attended the Wesleyan School in Sturminster Newton.

The eldest, Charles, was born in 1866, but very little seems to be known about him (Kenneth Topp has been unable to find any trace of a marriage or burial). Did he go to sea or emigrate?

The second child, James (1867-1913) went to Newfoundland, where in May 1890 at Brigus he married Mary Grace Way, whose family also originated from Dorset. James and his bride returned the same year to Dorset, where their only child, Ethel Amelia (Mae) was born. When Ethel was six years old, the family emigrated to Pennsylvania, U.S.A.

James was employed in the mines, where he was unfortunately killed in 1913, at the early age of forty-five. Mary Grace lived to the grand old age of ninety-three.

Their daughter Ethel (who died in 1975) married Edward J. Cooney and they had seven children. There are a

Mary Ann Topp, wife of Charles

James Topp, his wife Mary Grace and daughter Ethel Amelia (Mae)

number of descendants widely dispersed in the U.S.A.

The third child, Mary Ann Rolls Topp, born in 1870, subsequently lived in Lymington and Portsmouth, but no marriage has been traced. She died in 1958.

Woodlands Farm. Mary Ann Topp (mother) is standing outside the front door. Her two daughters, Mary Ann and Eliza, can be seen (faintly), one outside each of the windows

Eliza (born 1873) at Wareham Parish Church in June 1907 married George Herbert Dicker (born 1884), son of William John Dicker, a blacksmith of Sherborne. Nothing further is known about them.

Daniel Bright Topp, the youngest child, was born in 1874. It was he who helped his father, going with him to Poole to deliver meat. Daniel died in 1942, but it is not known whether he married or where he lived when he moved away from Fiddleford,

161

apart from the period 1898, when he was in the U.S.A. with his brother James, until 1913 when he returned to Dorset following James's death.

George Topp (1835-1931), Kenneth Topp's grandfather, was the second son of John and Eliza Topp, and younger brother of Charles of Woodlands Farm, Fiddleford. George lived and carried on his business as a master butcher and dairy farmer at a site overlooking The Green at Old Milton in Hampshire. The cottage, of 18th century origin, was demolished in the 1950's. In the early 19th century the parlour had been used as a Post Office. The butcher's shop, added by George Topp in 1860, survived until 1990, when it was demolished to make way for offices. The thatched slaughterhouse and stables with the picturesque front garden had disappeared in an earlier 20th century road widening scheme.

THE THATCHED COTTAGE, MILTON GREEN, OLD MILTON, HANTS.

Artist's Impression

162

George Topp married Sara Jane Crew (born 1839, died aged 81) at St. Andrew's church, Okeford Fitzpaine in March 1860. She was the third daughter of John Crew and Martha, nee Ridout (grand-daughter of Roger Ridout the smuggler).

Kenneth Topp says "John Crew was a miller, baker, farmer and innkeeper. He ran the Royal Oak at Okeford Fitzpaine from 1859 until 1867, so you can guess where my grandfather George met his bride to be!"

George Topp, 1839-1931

He (Kenneth) has an old photograph of his grandfather. He says "I took the original photograph of George Topp, in its little case, to the National Museum of Photography at Bradford some time ago and the Museum dated it mid 19c. As George was married . . . . . on the 19 March 1860 this confirmed that George had the photo' taken for his wedding . . . . .

At first the Museum said that the photographic process used for the photograph was Daguerreotype but had second thoughts and came to the conclusion that it must have been the wet Collodion process which superseded the Daguerreotype."

Louis Daguerre used silver plated copper plate coated with silver iodide as a light-sensitive surface. In his first experiments he co-operated with Joseph Nicephore Niepce, a retired French army officer, who had in 1827 produced the first successful photograph with pewter plates coated with bitumen, and developed with lavender oil and white petroleum. The exposure was eight hours, and the image, a view from his window, was somewhat blurred!

Daguerre cut the exposure time to an hour and, by 1841, to twenty seconds. There was no negative — the final picture was on the metal surface. The sitter sometimes had to remain absolutely motionless for maybe five or six minutes, perhaps enduring a concealed clamp to keep his head still! No wonder the facial expression was usually grim!

The Collodion process referred to by the Bradford Museum was invented in 1851 by F. Scott Archer. Glass plates were coated with collodion (a colourless, gummy liquid consisting of gun-cotton in ether) containing potassium and other iodides. Then, after being dipped into a solution of silver nitrate, the plates were exposed in the camera whilst still wet.

These early photographs (some of which — Daguerreotypes in particular — are now quite valuable and are collectors' items) were no doubt very expensive at the time, and the portrait of George Topp was probably, as his grandson suggests, a once-in-a-lifetime luxury taken on or near his wedding day.

There were other branches of the family in the area. Another George Topp (1814-1887), a yeoman farmer of 320 acres, lived at Styles Farm (named after George Style), which at one time was part of the glebe lands of Mappowder village.

Grade 2 listed, the house was built in the 17th century of coursed rubble. The square-headed 17th century windows can be seen on the west gable (on the right of the picture).

Artist's impression
C 1850
of Style's Farmhouse, Mappowder,
Co, Dorset

LIONEL SLATER

George Topp added the 19th century extension — the names of his four sons, George, John, Richard and Henry could be seen carved in the brickwork. The remains of the 17th century facade, including a stone arched entrance, are now concealed by the later work.

George was a descendant of John Topp (c. 1526-1589), yeoman farmer and butcher of Woodrow, Hazelbury Bryan. Born at Sturminster Newton, George married (in 1840) Mary Anne, daughter of Robert and Sarah Witteridge of Ibberton.

John Topp, father of George, for almost forty years farmed 165 acres at Puxey.

THE WESLEYAN CHAPEL

Two Steward's Books have now become available at the Dorset County Records Office. One [NM7:S11/TS 1/1] holds the very simple accounts for the years 1870 until 1916. The closing entry which reads *"Examined and found correct.* [signed] *Stuart Knight"*, is dated 19 February 1917.

The Chapel Treasurer's task was certainly not very time-consuming, as can be seen from the 1870 Balance Sheet:

1870	Disbursements	£	s	d		Receipts		£	s	d
Nov. 8	Paid for Oil etc.		10	5	March	First Quarter		1	2	6
	Paid to Quarter Board				June	Second Quarter		1	2	6
	Four Quarters				Sep	Third Quarter		1	2	6
	@ 10/-	2	0	0	Dec	Fourth Quarter		1	2	6
								4	10	0
1871										
March 1	Paid for painting		8	0						
March 8	Paid for Candles		13	6				3	11	11
		3	11	11		Balance in hand			18	1

Examined and found correct on this 7th day of March 1871
    F. Gwynne — Chairman
    Edward Jackson   } Auditors
    Asher Foot

The expenditure was low — very little was required in the Chapel, and the articles purchased most frequently were candles and oil. A modest amount was allowed for lighting, cleaning and *"warming"*.

A mat was acquired in 1871, for which 5s. 6d [27½p] was paid. In 1888 it seems as though some repair work was carried out:

1888

Income

Date	Description	£	s	d
	Balance in hand	1	0	4
	Balance received from Mr. Herrington proceeds of tea		11	4½
	For Seat Rents due Jan. 26 88	1	3	0
	" " " April 30 88		10	6
	" " " July 23 88		10	6
	" " " Oct 16 88	1	3	0
		4	18	8½

Expenditure

Date	Description	£	s	d
Jay. 6	Mr. F. Knotts Bill		12	0
	Mr. J. R. Cressey Bill 1 pane of glass		1	0
Paid to "	Quarter Board March 27		10	0
"	Quarter Board June 21		10	0
June	Mr. Bests Bill piping		3	0
Paid to	Quarter Board Sept. 27		8	0
Dec. 17	12 feet board for tressels @ 2d		2	0
" "	Lamps	1	2	6
Dec. 13	Paid to Quarter Board		8	0
	Repairing pulpit [deleted]		private payment	
" "	Mrs. Maidment's bill of oil		8	11
" "	Mrs. Maidment's cleaning chapel		2	0
		4	7	5
	Balance in hand carried forward		11	3½
		4	18	8½

For readers unfamiliar with the 'old' currency, 20s (shillings) or 240d (pence) made £1. 1/- (one shilling) equals 5p. 6d equals 2½p.

1892 was an expensive year because this was when the Chapel was moved on rollers from Mr. Wilds' garden (which was the garden of what is now called Manor Farm House) across the lane to a new site adjacent to Woodview. The accounts showed "Mr. J. R. Cresseys for Moving Chapel ect. [sic] as p. Bill £7. 5. 0." This apparently included painting and other work. Mr. J. Caines was paid £1. 0. 0. for brickwork and "Mr. Brennands Bill" amounted to £5. 6. 10. It must have been difficult for the Chapel to find this sum of money, but 'subscriptions' were received from Mr. Harvey £3, Mr. S. J. Cressey £1, a friend 10/-, Mr. Chadwick 5/-. Mr. Wilds 5/- and Mr. C. Elkins 2/-. A collection at a Tea Meeting held on 8 September 1892 added £1. 8. 10.

On the 28 September 1893 another Public Tea Meeting was held. Mr. Eaton was paid £1. 12. 1. for cake. Tea and sugar was brought by Mrs. S. Maidment (7/8d) and Mr. Furnell (5/2d). Mrs. Drake received 3/- for printing and Mr. Wilds 6/- for milk and butter. 1/- was charged for cleaning, making the total expenditure £2. 14. 11. Unfortunately the income was only £2. 13. 8, which included the collection, money for cakes sold, and presumably a small entrance fee!

In 1895 Mr. Barnett was paid £7. 10. 9 for a new fence. The harmonium was beginning to require attention, and in 1904 10/- was allocated "towards new harmonium". No further reference is made to purchasing a new instrument, but in 1908 10/- was paid for "repairing harmonium", and another 2/6d for the same purpose in 1912.

In 1905 13/- was spent on new hymn books for the pulpit and organ, and "Stove Pipe Repairs" cost 7/6d. In 1907 Mr. Barnett was paid 4/6d for a coal scuttle, hymn books cost 6/- and — a little luxury! — Mrs. Westcott received 6/5d for a fringe for the pulpit, and Mrs. Linklater 1/9 for "velvet for pulpit".

In 1916 there is an item of 1/- for "Brown Paper for Windows". The Chapel must have been closed for some reason, as, also in 1916, 2/- was paid for "Handbills re re-opening".

It appears that the Chapel was struggling financially from 1910 until 1916 as the income was always slightly less than the expenditure, but at the end of each year "a subscription" equivalent to the loss was received. When the Auditor signed the accounts on 19 February 1917 there was a deficit of 1/11d.

The second small Book [D.C.R.O. NM.7:S/11/TS 1/2] shows only one set of accounts for 1919, and at the end of that year there was a Balance in Hand of 13/1. A list of amounts of the collections at services is given for July 27 until October 12. The largest of these, on August 3, was 1/1½d and the smallest, on August 17, was 3d.

The Records Office also has a Collection Journal for Fiddleford Chapel [D.C.R.O. NM.7:S/11/TS 1/1]. This gives not only the amounts donated by the congregation in 1915, but also the recipients of the collections. About half were for the Methodist funds, but 1/11 was given to *"Worn Out Ministers"* on June 6, 1/8½d to *"Horse Hire Fund"* on June 27, 3/- to *"G. War Fund"* on October 31 and 1/11d to *"F. Missionary"* on November 28.

Eleven shillings accrued as a result of the Harvest Festival in 1917 — 2/1d in the afternoon, 1/11½d in the evening, 1/2½ on Tuesday and 5/9d from the sale of produce. Of this, 5/6d went to the Circuit and 5/6 was retained by the Chapel.

The Rev. E. Mortimer and the Rev. S. Knight took services during the period 1916/1917, in addition to local preachers — Messrs. Blandford, Burrows, D. Cutler, Fudge, Lanning, P. Lydford, Riggs, Sloper, Tizzard and Wallis.

The Dorset County Records Office has two documents showing that the Chapel was insured from September 1916 to September 1917, and again in the following year, with the Wesleyan Methodist Trust Assurance Company Limited, 38 Fountain Street, Manchester, under Fire Policy No. 27014. The Sum Insured was £50, and the annual premium 2/6d.
[D.C.R.O. NM7:S11/TS1/1]

170

EXTRACTS FROM COURT BOOKS

It seems that the most common complaints at the Manor Court were the failure of certain tenants to maintain the roadways and paths in good condition, or encroachment by tenants on to footways and common land, i.e. 'acquiring' an extra piece of land for themselves.

STURMINSTER NEWTON CASTLE COURT BOOK
[D.C.R.O. D.PIT/M.69]

21 October 1737. "They present that the Waywardens of Sturminster Newton have not amended the Lane sufficiently leading thro' Piddles Woods it is therefore ordered that the same be done before Christmas next on Pain of 10s.

"Southly is much in Decay and ought to be repaired by the Tennants who have Lands Adjacent thereunto in proportion to their Number of Acres it is therefore Ordered that the same be done within Six Months next ensueing on Pain of 6s. 8d [approx. 33p] each Person makeing Default."

*   *   *   *   *   *   *   *   *   *

STURMINSTER NEWTON COURT BOOK 1749-1759
[D.C.R.O. D/PIT M70]

25 October 1751

"Mr. William Baker for Moveing the Bounds in Southley Mead betwixt Joseph Sweets and his own Ground. It is therefore ordered by this Court that the Incroachment be thrown out again within Seven Days Space on Pain of Ten Shillings."

*   *   *   *   *   *   *   *   *   *

26 October 1753, 22 October 1755, 28 October 1757 — on all these occasions the "way leading to Southley Mead much out of repair".

*   *   *   *   *   *   *   *   *   *

STURMINSTER NEWTON COURT BOOK
[D.C.R.O. D/PIT.M71]

1762 List or Rate of Law-day Silver due from the suitors of Newton tything yearly payable at the Public Court . . . . .

Margt. Matchams living	0.	0.	2½
Ben. Belbin for Dibbens	0.	0.	6
Town Mills (John Newman) this paymt Disputed	0.	0.	6
Joshua Rose	0.	0.	2½
The late Wm. Crews	0.	0.	5
Piddles Wood	0.	0.	6
Fiddleford Farm (Colber Tithg.)	0.	0.	6
Wid. Churchill's living	0.	0.	2½
Robt. Goodfellows living	0.	0.	6
Mrs. Mary Belbin	0.	0.	2½
John Newmans Ho.	0.	0.	2½

* * * * * * * * * *

OKEFORD FITZPAINE COURT BOOK No. 4 — 1771-1790
[D.C.R.O. D/PIT.M62]

Page 36. Court Baron 20 October 1779

"They present Robert Goodfellow hath made an encroachment on the Highway near his Dwellinghouse at Fiddleford within this Manor by erecting posts and taking in a footway out of the Highway there whereby waggons passing that road are greatly interrupted. Ordered that the footway be laid open to the waggon road within one Month from the date hereof Under the Penalty of Ten Pounds."

* * * * * * * * * *

STURMINSTER NEWTON COURT BOOK
[D.C.R.O. D.PIT/M71]

Sturminster Newton Court 16 October 1780

They present the Bridge over a deep Ditch out of Southley Mead into the Field next to Fiddleford Mill in the Foot Road from Sturminster to Blandford as unsafe for Passengers, there being no Rail to it, and the Water sometimes penning up very high out of the River, there is likewise a deep Hole at the End of the said Bridge in Southley Mead so that a person must sometimes be

172

knee high in Water to get to it. Ordered that there be a Rail put, and the said Hole filled up by the Person or Persons to whom it belongs, within a Month from the Date hereof under Penalty of twenty Shillings."

* * * * * * * * * *

The footbridge as it is today (photographed by Irene Thomas)

Sturminster Court   27 October 1783

"They present the Bridge over the Brook at Fiddleford in the Foot Road from Sturminster to Blandford very dangerous for Passengers the Ground or Earth being gone at the hither End of the Bridge that there is no getting to it when the Water is up. Ordered to be repaired within a Month from the Date hereof by the Person or Persons to whom it belongs under the Penalty of Twenty Shillings."

Sturminster Court   27 October 1785

"They present the Bridge in the Foot Road from Sturminster to Blandford over a deep Ditch near the River out of Southley Mead towards Fiddleford Mill, where the water sometimes pens up to a considerable Height, unsafe for Passengers in the Night, as there is no Rail to it. Ordered that there be a Rail put within a Month from the Date hereof by the Person to whom it belongs under the Penalty of Twenty Shillings."

* * * * * * * * * *

OKEFORD FITZPAINE COURT BOOK No. 4 — 1771-1790
[D.C.R.O. D/PIT.M.62]

Page 58   20 October 1784

"William Adams be continued Hayward for Fiddleford Mead for the year ensuing."

* * * * * * * * * *

Page 72   20 October 1788

". . . . the Maypole is a nuisance — ordered that the same be taken down immediately" [presumably the Maypole in Okeford Fitzpaine village]

* * * * * * * * * *

STURMINSTER NEWTON COURT BOOK
[D.C.R.O. D.PIT/M71]

4 July 1788

A Rate made and assessed by the Churchwardens and overseers of the Poor for the relief of the Poor being the fifth Rate for one month from the Date hereof.

Charles Andrews for Fiddleford Farm	£1.	0. 6
Priscilla Newman for her House	0.	0. 6
John Newman Junr. for Bucks	0.	2. 0
John Newman Junr. for Huniberts	0.	1. 6
John Newman Junr. for Fiddleford Mills	0.	1. 6
William Stanley for Gurdleys Copse	0.	1. 0

* * * * * * * * * *

OKEFORD FITZPAINE COURT BOOK No. 4 — 1771-1790

[D.C.R.O. D.PIT/M62]

Page 79   6 October 1790

"James Shrimpton has neglected to Repair the Gate of Fiddleford Mead, according to the antient Custom of this Manor, in right of his Land adjoining thereto. It is ordered that the same be put into good Repair by the said James Shrimpton in ten days under the penalty of Forty Shillings."

* * * * * * * * * *

STURMINSTER NEWTON COURT BOOK

[D.C.R.O. D.PIT/M.72]

Sturminster Court   22 October 1801

"They present the foot Road going out of John Strange's Field into Samuel Dawson's Field being the Foot Road from Newton to Fiddleford to be in bad repair and very dangerous for people to pass. Ordered to be repaired * in the course of a Month under the penalty of Twenty Shillings."   * Inserted above, in different ink, "thought to be repaired by John Strange."

* * * * * * * * * *

OKEFORD FITZPAINE COURT BOOK 1808-1854

[D.C.R.O. D/PIT.M.63]

Court Baron   12 October 1819

"John and Richard Osmond have lately take in and Inclosed a piece of Ground at Fiddleford within this Manor opposite their Cottages on the other side of the Road ordered that the same be thrown out within six Months under the penalty of Twenty Shillings."

RUNAWAY APPRENTICES

On the 4th May 1778 an item concerning two runaway apprentices from Okeford Fitzpaine appeared in the Sherborne Mercury.

"Whereas WILLIAM FUDGE and ROBERT NEWMAN, apprentices to Mr. Roger Hames of Okeford Fitzpain, cordwainer, have, without any provocation eloped from their said master, and have, after repeated applications, refused to return and serve out their time. This, therefore, is to inform any of his Majesty's officers or soldiers or sailors, if they will take them into custody, to serve his Majesty in either, shall, on applying as above, have their indentures given up. And if any person harbours or employs them in any other way; after this date, shall be prosecuted as the law directs.

William Fudge is about 5 feet 10 inches high, thin made, wore his own black hair, and is about 18 or 19 years of age, and is now somewhere between Weymouth and Bridport.

Robert Newman is near the make of Fudge, and is now in Blandford, Dorset.

April 30, 1778"

There is no way of knowing exactly where in the parish of Okeford Fitzpaine Roger Hames lived, but there were families of Hames, Fudge and Newman in Fiddleford in the 19th century.

John Hilliar

This photograph was taken c. 1915 in Castle Lane, outside the cottage in which he lived

OKEFORD FITZPAINE SCHOOLS

Previous research regarding schools at Okeford Fitzpaine revealed little information about the location of such establishments prior to the 1841 Census Return.

An anonymous, undated document [D.C.R.O. PE/OFP. SC1-3] discovered at the Dorset County Records Office described a ceremony at which two cottages were conveyed to the Rev. G. R. Hunter on condition that they were rebuilt and used as a Sunday School and Village School [W.E.T.G. Page 198].

The Rev. Hunter was Rector of Okeford from December 1820 until May 1872, and it was thought probable that the cottages concerned were on the site of the house (called School House) in the centre of the village. There appeared to be nothing to connect the details in the statement about the conveyance with the words written on the envelope which contained it . . . "1838 - Greenhay".

But it now seems that there was a schoolmaster (and perhaps a school) at Greenhay nearly three hundred years before the above events took place. Is it coincidence that Greenhay is mentioned in both cases? Or was there some connection? We shall probably never know.

Mr. Robin Rendell of Bedfont, Middlesex has found (in Suffolk and Norfolk) documents which relate to his ancestors who lived in or near Okeford Fitzpaine. He says:

"My ancestors came from Okeford Fitzpaine — they went under the surname of Raynoldes alias Hiscock. Either name or both were used. The first I have proved, with documentary evidence, was Henry (1563), a schoolmaster at Greenhay, Okeford Fitzpaine.

My ancestors remained in Okeford Fitzpaine well into the mid-1700's. A will of that date (1732) shows John Raynold leaving Linceys Farm in Okeford Fitzpaine to his children.

Henry Raynolde, schoolmaster, of Greenhay had a brother Roger — both held land in Okeford Fitzpaine, Durweston and Shillingstone, 1560/1590. Roger's son, Richard, grew grapes and apples in Durweston. A document I have says "*I loaded a whole waggon of apples in hoggshead at Reynoldes farm in Durweston bound for Blandford and the carte nearly fell over. The apples were going to Barnard Mitchells of London.*" (1658)

[Dorchester Museum — Pope & Fry from original at P.R.O.]

In 1655 another ancestor called Henry Raynolde was the "*church record keeper*" in Okeford Fitzpaine. It appears from the 1580's through to the late 1600's my ancestors were church guardians. Roger of Durweston and Okeford Fitzpaine was also a tything man and various documents I have copies of show local 'Pimperne Hundred' courts where local issues were decided, one that comes to mind being a court held in Hazelbury Bryan. The case mentions William Strangeway, gent, fined for allowing the byeway '*to become obnoxious with puddles*'. Another tells of Robert Harte drawing blood from John Mow with a stick [1579 Pimperne Court]."

The document [HA52877], dated 1563, showing H. Reynold of Greenhay, Okeford Fitzpaine as "*ludi m*" (i.e. ludimagister — schoolmaster) is one in a collection of Sir Thomas Kitson's papers at Suffolk County Records Office.

Two further items in Sir Thomas Kitson's accounts show, in 1580, Henry Reynold renting "*Greenhay al* [alias] *Playing Close*" [S.C.R.O. HA528] and in 1587 "*Henrye Reynolde tooke the reversion of one tnem* [tenement] *with appurtenances in Okeforde ffitzpaine aforesaid which the saide Henrye lately helde and paied ffine £8*" [S.C.R.O. E3/15/53/3.1]

Mr. Rendell sent a transcript of a document dated 1592 [S.C.R.O. E3/15/53/3.2] which granted "*to John Raynolde and Henry Raynolde the reversion of one tenement with appurtenances which Henry Raynolde their father doth hold for the ffyne of ? to be paid at Michaelmas next.*"

Obviously the Reynold family was active in Okeford Fitzpaine for at least two hundred years. It would be interesting to know a little more about *"H. Reynold"* who, in 1563, ran a small school or perhaps was a private tutor at his cottage in Greenhay.

THE LODER FAMILY

Information has come to hand about the Loders of Okeford Fitzpaine from Iris Loder of Swanage, whose husband's ancestors lived in the village from around 1727 until 1925. She has more to add to the rather sketchy details previously available about the two ladies called Mrs. Loder, both of whom were schoolmistresses in the village in the nineteenth century.

She says, "The Loders seem to have come to Okeford Fitzpaine about 1727 and brought a son WILLIAM with them — first entry in register is baptism of THOMAS 1728.

The schoolmistress Mary Loder was the second wife of George Loder, and Harriet was her step-daughter. Mary (age 9) was, as they said then, 'Base Born'.

Martha Loder (nee Stickland) was the second wife of Louis Loder (who was the above George's son). Rather extraordinary both father and son should have schoolmistresses as their second wives."

Mrs. Loder supplied a 'Tree' [on the following two pages] which may be of interest to other people from Okeford Fitzpaine who are trying to trace a family line.

Mrs. Loder continues "My husband's grandfather, George [son of Louis] was also Parish Clerk like his father. He was a carpenter and wheelwright and lived in Wistaria Cottage, where my husband's father was born in 1879 (and three sisters). He left Okeford in 1925 when his wife died, and lived with his daughter in London until his death in 1934. He is buried in Okeford churchyard.

My husband's father, Louis William was sent to school in London at 12, lived with his uncle Anthony Rose in New Cross and subsequently worked in his uncle's firm, A. Rose & Co., Wool Brokers in Bermondsey, and seldom returned to Okeford.

181

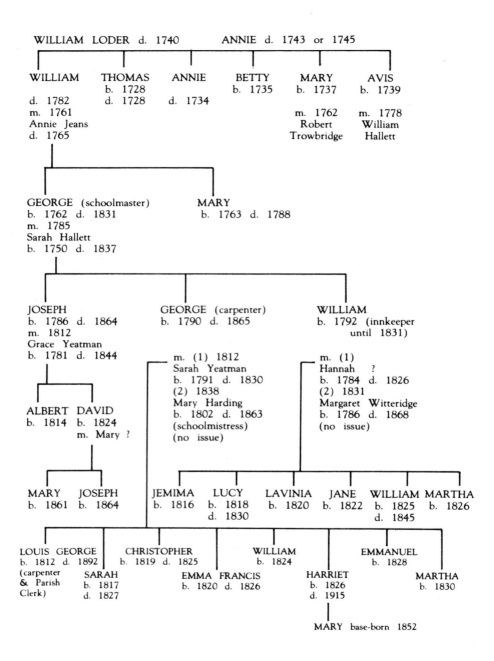

WILLIAM LODER d. 1740   ANNIE d. 1743 or 1745

WILLIAM
d. 1782
m. 1761
Annie Jeans
d. 1765

THOMAS
b. 1728
d. 1728

ANNIE
d. 1734

BETTY
b. 1735

MARY
b. 1737
m. 1762
Robert
Trowbridge

AVIS
b. 1739
m. 1778
William
Hallett

GEORGE (schoolmaster)
b. 1762 d. 1831
m. 1785
Sarah Hallett
b. 1750 d. 1837

MARY
b. 1763 d. 1788

JOSEPH
b. 1786 d. 1864
m. 1812
Grace Yeatman
b. 1781 d. 1844

GEORGE (carpenter)
b. 1790 d. 1865

WILLIAM
b. 1792 (innkeeper
until 1831)

m. (1) 1812
Sarah Yeatman
b. 1791 d. 1830
(2) 1838
Mary Harding
b. 1802 d. 1863
(schoolmistress)
(no issue)

m. (1)
Hannah ?
b. 1784 d. 1826
(2) 1831
Margaret Witteridge
b. 1786 d. 1868
(no issue)

ALBERT
b. 1814

DAVID
b. 1824
m. Mary ?

MARY
b. 1861

JOSEPH
b. 1864

JEMIMA
b. 1816

LUCY
b. 1818
d. 1830

LAVINIA
b. 1820

JANE
b. 1822

WILLIAM
b. 1825
d. 1845

MARTHA
b. 1826

LOUIS GEORGE
b. 1812 d. 1892
(carpenter
& Parish
Clerk)

SARAH
b. 1817
d. 1827

CHRISTOPHER
b. 1819 d. 1825

EMMA
b. 1820

FRANCIS
d. 1826

WILLIAM
b. 1824

HARRIET
b. 1826
d. 1915

EMMANUEL
b. 1828

MARTHA
b. 1830

MARY base-born 1852

182

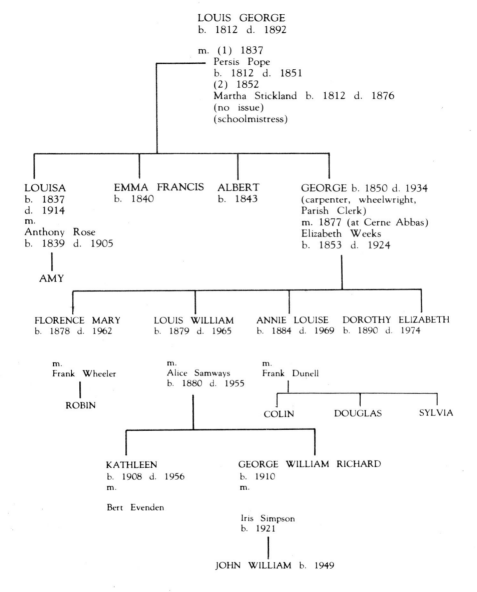

LOUIS GEORGE
b. 1812 d. 1892

m. (1) 1837
Persis Pope
b. 1812 d. 1851
(2) 1852
Martha Stickland b. 1812 d. 1876
(no issue)
(schoolmistress)

LOUISA
b. 1837
d. 1914
m.
Anthony Rose
b. 1839 d. 1905

AMY

EMMA FRANCIS
b. 1840

ALBERT
b. 1843

GEORGE b. 1850 d. 1934
(carpenter, wheelwright,
Parish Clerk)
m. 1877 (at Cerne Abbas)
Elizabeth Weeks
b. 1853 d. 1924

FLORENCE MARY
b. 1878 d. 1962

LOUIS WILLIAM
b. 1879 d. 1965

ANNIE LOUISE
b. 1884 d. 1969

DOROTHY ELIZABETH
b. 1890 d. 1974

m.
Frank Wheeler

m.
Alice Samways
b. 1880 d. 1955

m.
Frank Dunell

ROBIN

COLIN   DOUGLAS   SYLVIA

KATHLEEN
b. 1908 d. 1956
m.

Bert Evenden

GEORGE WILLIAM RICHARD
b. 1910
m.

Iris Simpson
b. 1921

JOHN WILLIAM b. 1949

Anthony Rose (baptised Sturminster Newton 1839) was the son of Samuel Rose (baptised Okeford Fitzpaine 1812) and his wife Mary (nee Phillips).

There was a previous George Loder (1762-1831) in the family who was stated to be a Schoolmaster in his will, so there could have been a school of some sort in Okeford in the early 1800's."

JOHN HILLIAR

(Entries in the Parish Registers show the name as Hillier, Hellyar, Hellyer, Hillyar, Hilliar — the spellings given below are as written in the various Registers.)

John Hillier was born in Okeford Fitzpaine and baptised at the Parish Church on 16 June 1822. He was one of the children of James Hillier and his wife Susannah (nee Goffe), who were married at St. Andrew's Church on 26 July 1813.

On 23 September 1851 John (Helyar) married Elizabeth Rose, daughter of Richard Rose, a labourer. They lived in Castle Lane, opposite the Recreation Ground, in a house now called Castle Cottage, and he carried on his trade as a carpenter in a workshop in his garden. Elizabeth died in January 1899 at the age of 75. John lived another eighteen years, and was buried on 13 January 1917, aged 97.

John and Elizabeth had seven sons and one daughter. With the exception of a boy who died at the age of five, they were brought up in the village. As mentioned in Where Elm Trees Grew, one of the sons was Thomas (baptised 10 February 1856) who, keen to learn to read and write, became one of Martha Loder's pupils at Wistaria Cottage. He went there to school in the evenings once or twice a week after finishing work.

Eventually Tom Hilliar became the miller at Okeford Fitzpaine, taking over in 1886 and remaining until the mill ceased to operate, which, says his daughter Nellie, was c.1920.

Wistaria Cottage — date unknown (probably early 20th century)

In the latter part of the 19th century a young Swiss lady, Anna Kiener, was engaged by the family at Turnworth House to teach the three daughters French, German, Spanish and Italian. Anna was eighteen years old when she came to England, intending herself to benefit from her employment by improving her knowledge of the English language. In 1888 she married Thomas Hilliar.

Thomas and Anna brought up their family of nine children at Okeford Mill house, where they lived until 1932. Tom Hilliar was buried in November 1942 at the age of 86 — the Register of Burials records that his address at the time of his death was Rose Hill Farm. Anna was living in Castle Avenue when she died, aged 88, in February 1956.

Frank, one of their sons who was born in 1894, left school at fourteen to help his father in the mill. He lived in

Thomas Hilliar and Anna Kiener on their wedding day, 17 October 1888

Okeford Fitzpaine all his life, leaving only to fight in the 1914-18 war. He was a versatile man, being able to sing Dorset songs and recite Dorset poetry in dialect to appreciative audiences in the village. He was a bell-ringer, and also composed songs, one of which he recorded (privately, in 1974) on tape. This was about the happy love affair of a young lady and her future husband, Billy Gray, who every Sunday evening before their marriage met and (not surprisingly) *"strolled by the river, down by the mill"*. Adjacent to Frank's home was a building which housed all the equipment necessary for cider-making in the old traditional way — grinder, press, casks etc., and Frank applied himself to this enjoyable task every autumn when the apples were ready. He died in 1982.

Nellie (now Mrs. Bert Ridout), one of Thomas and Anna Hilliar's daughters, still lives in Okeford Fitzpaine with her husband.

Anna Hilliar (right) and her daughter Edie in the garden of Okeford Mill House

James and Susan Lydford

WESLEYAN DAY SCHOOL STURMINSTER NEWTON

Mr. Walter Wilkins was a well-known and very respected Headmaster who was in charge of the Wesleyan Day School at Sturminster Newton from 1875 until 1913. Known as 'Daddy', he was a strict disciplinarian, but made sure that his pupils received a good education.

Back Row: Richard, William, Ethelbert, D'Arcy (Mrs. Thomas's father) and Percy
Middle Row: May Selby (nee Lydford), Rose, Eva Perry (nee Lydford),
Lily Cowley (nee Lydford), and Laura Norrell (nee Lydford)
Seated at front: James and Susan Lydford   (Photo c.1912)

On Page 227 of Where Elm Trees Grew is a copy of a letter written by James and Susan Lydford to Mr. Wilkins, thanking him *"for the very efficient and painstaking way you have instructed the whole of our family . . . ."* This family consisted of five sons and five daughters, the first of whom started at the school in 1881. The last left in 1912, so that one or more of the Lydford children attended the school *"for a period extending over 31 years. The length of time our children have received instruction from you works out to a total of about 100 years, or an average for each child being about 10 years . . . ."* Mr. and Mrs. Lydford wondered whether any other family had *"a better record than ours".*

Irene Thomas (nee Lydford), a grandchild of James and Susan Lydford, is known for her books of poems published under her pseudonym 'a Dosset Maid'. Mrs. Thomas has supplied two photographs of Mr. and Mrs. James Lydford, one with the 'five sons and five daughters' referred to in the letter dated 29th August 1912.

AUSTRALIA — FIRST FREE SETTLERS

It is exactly two hundred years since a small party left England in 1792 to start a new life on the other side of the world. They were the first voluntary emigrants to Australia.

More than four years earlier, in January 1788, with Captain Arthur Phillip in charge, eleven ships of the First Fleet had reached Sydney Cove, New South Wales, with the initial wave of convicts transported for various offences, some of which today would be considered minor. Soldiers escorted them throughout the voyage and supervised during the setting up of the penal colony after their arrival. Conditions were tough, and, as supplies had to be brought by ship, food was at first inadequate. Some of the convicts, perhaps those who were hardened criminals and no doubt resentful of their fate, were not good workers. Arthur Phillip petitioned repeatedly for free settlers to be brought from England, since *"fifty farmers would do more to render the colony independent than a thousand convicts"*.

Various inducements, such as free passage, tools and implements, two years' provisions and one year's clothing, must have proved attractive to those considering leaving England. They would also have the opportunity to use convict labour in their new homeland.

And so on 8 August 1792 the square rigged vessel Bellona, 472 tons, with Matthew Boyd (her Master) in command, set sail from Gravesend.

More than half of the emigrants on board came from Sturminster Newton. They were:

Thomas Rose	40		farmer
Jane Rose (nee Topp)	33	his wife	
Thomas Rose	13	son	
Mary Rose	11	daughter	
Joshua Rose	9	son	
Richard Rose	3	son	
Elizabeth Fish	18	niece of Thomas Rose	
Elizabeth Watts	18	probably a servant	

The rest of the party were:

Frederick Meredith	single	baker
Thomas Webb		gardener
Joseph Webb	18 nephew, single	farmer
Walter Brodie		blacksmith
Edward Powell	30	farmer & fisherman of Lancaster
James Thorpe		millwright

Thomas Rose, born in 1749, was the son of Christopher Rose and his wife Mary (nee Belbin). Mary was the niece of Rose Pitt (nee Belbin) who lived for many years at Fiddleford (see Page 86). So Fiddleford can claim a tenuous connection with the first free settlers in Australia.

Jane Rose was the eldest child of Thomas Topp (1729-1801), a yeoman farmer and master butcher in Bridge Street, Sturminster Newton. He was also Councillor-Governor of the Sturminster Poor House. Mary Topp, his wife, was a home spinner.

Thomas Rose and Jane Topp married at Sturminster Newton on 8 August 1779.

When, on 15 January 1793 after a voyage of five months, they set foot on Australian soil at Sydney Cove, Arthur Phillip, the man who had urged the government to encourage them to come, was already on his way back to England, having left in December because of ill health.

Shortly after their arrival, Thomas Rose's niece, Elizabeth Fish (1774-1836) married Edward Powell in Sydney, and Thomas Webb married a convict, Catherine Buckley on 24 January 1793.

Land at a place they called Liberty Plains (now Strathfield-Homebush), a few miles from Sydney Cove, was allocated to the men. Thomas Rose received 120 acres, Frederick Meredith 60 acres, Thomas Webb 80 acres, Joseph Webb 60 acres and Edward Powell (1762-1814) 80 acres. Walter Brodie stayed at

Sydney Cove as a blacksmith, whilst James Thorpe worked at the settlement mill.

In July Jane Rose was delivered of her fifth child — a son, John. He had the distinction of being the first baby to be born to free white settlers in the colony. By 1797 two more children — Sarah and Henry — had been added to Thomas and Jane's family.

Tragedy struck two of the group. Joseph Webb died in November 1794 when he was in his early twenties. This was followed only four months later by the death of his uncle, Thomas Webb, from one or more spear-wounds inflicted by aborigines belonging to the Daruk tribe. The murder resulted in the establishment of a military presence in the locality in 1796.

Poor soil and ignorance of local conditions caused hardship to the small band of settlers and Thomas Rose eventually moved to Wilberforce in the Hawkesbury district, where the land was more fertile. It is interesting that George Matcham Pitt, a grandson of Mary Pitt of Fiddleford who went to Australia in 1801, was born "on the farm on the Hawkesbury River, a grant in 1802 to his father Thomas". [See Mary Pitt (nee Matcham) — Page 23]

Severe floods devastated the area in 1806 and 1809 and Thomas Rose lost everything. After the second disaster he moved to the outskirts of Wilberforce, where he acquired 30 acres of land above reach of the floods. Here, on higher ground, he made his permanent home. It was a simple cottage built of split iron-bark slabs coated with a mixture of cow manure, wattle and clay. In the 1850's a covering of galvanised iron was added as protection for the roof, which was of split shingles laid on pit sawn rafters. There was one large living room, about twenty feet square, a kitchen and a bedroom. The children slept in an attic in the roof. Apparently the first Methodist meeting in Australia was held in the large room in 1816.

Called Rose Cottage, it was occupied by members of Thomas's family until 1961, the last being his great-great-grandson John. Thomas died 15 November 1833 at the age of 80, six years after Jane's death on 26 December 1827. Both were buried in

St. John's churchyard, Wilberforce. His obituary is one of which the present inhabitants of Sturminster Newton should be proud — *"Quiet, homely, unassuming and industrious, Thomas Rose belonged to that humble band of men who, in a rough and licentious age, helped to lay the foundations of ordered social life in a new country."*

Many descendants of Thomas and Jane are still living in Australia. In 1827, when Jane died, the Sydney Gazette (7 January 1828) reported that her descendants *"are supposed to number 100 individuals and upwards"*. If this were the case, they can probably now be counted in thousands.

Rose Cottage today is open to the public, and is part of a Pioneer Village. It is allegedly the oldest timber house in Australia, and attracts many tourists.

Conditions were rigorous not only in Australia but also in England at the end of the 18th century. Kenneth Topp has (by courtesy of the Mitchell Library of New South Wales) seen a copy of a letter written from Sturminster Newton by Thomas and Mary Topp to their daughter and son-in-law Jane and Thomas Rose.

Dated 10 March 1798 it reads *". . . . . . The times in England are verey hasardous and eavery thing is very dear, and eavery week threttn'd with a invasion by the French and wee believe it will shurely be so, as they are fully intended to invade this Cuntry . . . . The taxes heare are hardly to be borne, they are so heavy a tax opon saddle horses, three guineas [£3.15p] a year, sixteen shillings [80p] pon each cart horse, *clocks & watches. Stamps pon gloves and hatts, butter now 11d p pound. Beefe good 6d [2½p] pound. Oardinary cheese £1. 10s. od. pr hundw't, a hard tax pon dogs. They talk pon taxing the cows, and many other taxes to tedious to mention."*

*Clocks were taxed at 5/- [25p]; gold watches 10/- [50p]; silver or metal watches 3/6 [17p].

Could it be that this letter with news about an impending invasion by Napoleon's army prompted Thomas and Joshua, the two eldest sons of Thomas and Jane, to think about coming to England — a journey they made in the early 1800's? Apparently they travelled to this country in about 1803, and rumour has it that they joined the English volunteers gathered to meet the anticipated French attack. Thomas and Joshua went back to Australia after a few years.

Acknowledgements:
Roses From The South, by Ruth Sawley
Dorset and Australia 1788-1988 (Dorset Year Book 1989), by Kenneth Topp
The Rose Family of the Bellona, published by The Thomas & Jane Rose Society of Australia

Child Okeford —

Notice is hereby given that a Vestry or Meeting of the Rate Payers of this Parish will be held at the usual place on Thursday the twentieth day of — April instant at the Hour of ten in the forenoon for the purpose of consenting to or dissenting from the Sale of a Cottage and Garden in Gobson Common belonging to this Parish to Job Trowbridge who is now the Tenant thereof Dated this 15th day of April 1843 —

G. R. Baverstock
Wm Coombs } *Churchwardens*
E. Rossiter } *Overseers*

At a Meeting of the Rate Payers of said Parish of Child Okeford in — Vestry assembled at the Parish Church

on Thursday the Twentieth day of April instant in pursuance of the above Notice.

Present

Wm Coombs
Robert Baldwin }
John Rossiter }

{ E. Rossiter
{ J. Baverstock
{ Robert Haidway

It was resolved that Robert Baldwin be appointed Chairman.

Resolved further that this Meeting do unanimously consent to the Sale of the Cottage and Garden particularly referred to in the above Notice to the said Job Trowbridge at the sum of Thirty two pounds and two shillings, That the consent of this Meeting to such Sale be signified to the Poor Law Commissioners and that The Board of Guardians of the Sturminster Union do obtain the concurrence of the said

Poor Law Commissioners and convey and transfer the said Cottage and Garden to the said Job Trowbridge accordingly.

Signed on behalf of the Meeting.

— Chairman

Minutes of Vestry Meeting, Child Okeford 1843 [D.C.R.O. PE/CHO/VE1]
[Thanks to the Vicar and Parochial Parish Council of Child Okeford]

[See Page 199, paragraph 1]

MORE AUSTRALIAN SETTLERS

In 1798, when Thomas and Mary Topp of Sturminster Newton wrote to their daughter Jane in Australia, pay for the working class was outrageously low in comparison with the high cost of food, and numerous taxes had been imposed during the Napoleonic Campaigns. Dorset was notorious for its treatment of agricultural labourers, and eventually the exploitation of the poor by the landowners culminated in a struggle by the men of Tolpuddle to obtain a fair and reasonable wage.

In 1833, headed by George Loveless, they formed a Friendly Society and took a vow of secrecy. Although Friendly Societies were legal, the oath was not. Loveless and five more of the men were brought to court. A naval mutiny during the Napoleonic Wars had resulted in a law concerning secret societies being passed in 1797. Although the conflict between England and France had terminated some years previously, it was with breaking this law that the men were charged. George Loveless and his colleagues were found guilty and their sentence was transportation to Australia for seven years.

The six were victims of harsh employers and a blatantly prejudiced judge and jury. The events leading up to the trial were that the farmers had promised to pay the labourers a weekly wage of 10/- [50p]. The pledge was broken, and the men received only nine shillings, this being subsequently reduced to eight [40p]. The Vicar of Tolpuddle had presided over the meeting at which the ten shilling wage was agreed, but he denied any knowledge of it. The judiciary rightly declared that they no longer had any responsibility for fixing wages. The farmers were thus given a free hand. They promptly lowered the wage to seven shillings [35p] per week, threatening to reduce it still further to six shillings.

Public outcry at the sentences passed was such that, in 1836, the Martyrs were granted free pardons and passage back to England, although it was not until the following year that George Loveless arrived in this country. The return of the others was delayed even longer.

197

Dorchester (where the trial took place) and Tolpuddle are, of course, not far from Sturminster Newton. These events were taking place whilst Reuben Rose, fifth and youngest son of Benjamin Rose and his wife Sarah (nee Fish), was a teenager, and they must have made a profound impression on a boy of that age. The impact was probably enhanced by the fact that his father was an agricultural labourer, and Reuben too had just started to work on the land. Four sisters born after Reuben completed the family, and it must indeed have been a hard struggle for the parents to support themselves and their nine children.

Although another fifteen years were to pass before Reuben and his wife eventually left England for Australia, did the idea first enter his mind at this time? The original free settlers had left Sturminster Newton forty-two years earlier, in 1792, and, although there is no reason to believe that Thomas and Jane Rose were related to Reuben's family, news of their new life on the other side of the world was probably common knowledge in Sturminster Newton.

Reuben was born in July 1819 and baptised at Okeford Fitzpaine (his parents were living at Garlands Farm at the time). In July 1843 he married Hannah Jeanes at Stalbridge, where she had been born on 13 November 1821. Reuben was a labourer, and even before the arrival of two children (Edward 1843 and Sarah 1844) life must have been very unrewarding on the low wages and high prices prevalent at the time. With little chance of improving his status, and reports of the much better conditions in Australia, it is not surprising that Reuben and Hannah decided to leave their home and relatives in Sturminster Newton and begin a new life in another country.

Fiddleford has a double link with this family of emigrants from Sturminster Newton. Reuben's father, Benjamin Rose, was an older brother of James who married Charlotte Fudge at Sturminster Newton in August 1811. Job Rose (1812-1871), firstborn of James and Charlotte and miller of Fiddleford Mill, was Reuben's first cousin.

The second connection is through Reuben's sister Sarah, who married Thomas Trowbridge. They lived at Gobson (alias Banbury) Common with their children, one of whom was called Reuben. All the Census Returns from 1841 until the recently published ones of 1891 show Trowbridge families at Gobson Common, and it is probable that they were related. In 1843 at a Vestry Meeting of Ratepayers of Child Okeford parish, a resolution was passed consenting to the sale of a cottage and garden in Gobson Common to Job Trowbridge, who was then the tenant.

By 1861 Thomas and Sarah had eight children, and the 1871 Census shows two more sons. Thomas Trowbridge was an agricultural labourer and most of his sons worked on the land when they were old enough, so life could not have been easy for them. Did Sarah ever think of her brother in Australia and wish that she and her family could start afresh in a country where there were opportunities for those prepared to take them? By 1881 Sarah was a widow and at 59 years of age was recorded as *"a quilter"*. Sarah lived at Fiddleford for about forty years, but when the 1891 Census was recorded her name was missing and the only members of the large family still living at Gobson Common were Sarah's seventh child (third son) Thomas, his wife and baby son.

Reuben and Hannah Rose left Plymouth on board the ship Prince Regent, a barque of 528 tons, in early April 1849. The steerage passengers were 46 married couples, 50 single males, 36 single females, 92 children and 10 babies. Conditions were cramped, rations of food basic and water barely adequate. What a relief it must have been when they arrived in South Australia on 20 July 1849!

They disembarked at Adelaide. What Reuben did and where he lived immediately after his arrival is unknown. The family must have settled fairly soon at Glen Osmond, four miles south-east of Adelaide, their home when Hannah gave birth to their third child, Benjamin, in May 1850. More children followed — Reuben 1851, Joseph Henry 1854, Daniel 1855, Rhoda Rebecca 1856, William 1859 and Mary Elizabeth 1861.

Mining and agriculture were the two main sources of employment. As Reuben had come from a farming community in England, it is not surprising that he chose agricultural work in South Australia. In 1853 he was living in Fullarton, and it was in this village that he bought his first piece of land for £18. It measured 99 feet by 105 feet [approx. 30m x 32m].

He moved to the Macclesfield area, signed several leases and entered into various partnerships (all associated with farming) over the ensuing years. In 1870, in spite of the fact that he had just signed a lease for 67 acres, land which came into his ownership in 1879 and which he eventually sold in 1885, the family made a complete break and moved to Moonta. Copper had been discovered here in 1860/1 and it seems that Reuben spent the rest of his life at Moonta in labouring jobs associated with the mines. In a letter to his son Edward he wrote in July 1879 *"I have still work sometimes in the stables sometimes on the flours . . . "* The reference to *"flours"* probably meant *"floors"* — employment in the mines where the ore was processed on two floors.

Throughout the easy and the less affluent times, Reuben, like his cousin Job Rose in England, remained an active Methodist and was a lay preacher. After his death in September 1886 at the age of 67 a lengthy obituary, written by two well-known Methodist Ministers, appeared in the Primitive Methodist Record dated January 1887.

Among the tributes is the phrase *"Few men have been more loved than Reuben Rose."* The article continues *"I knew him well and respected him highly, both for what he was in himself and for the services he rendered to our divine Master's cause. He was a man of kindly spirit, tender, sympathetic and generous. He was a genuine christian . . . . . No wonder that he was so greatly respected and loved in his life, and went down to the grave amid general regret . . . . ."* [part of the In Memoriam printed in Ruth Sawley's book Roses From The South]

Hannah had died, aged 59, in July 1880, six years before Reuben passed away. They are buried in the same grave at Moonta cemetery.

Many of their descendants still live in Australia, and their families and fortunes have been described in great detail in her books Roses From The South and its supplement Roses All The Way by Ruth Sawley, a direct descendant of Reuben and Hannah Rose, and to whom acknowledgement is made for the material used in the latter (Australian) part of this chapter.

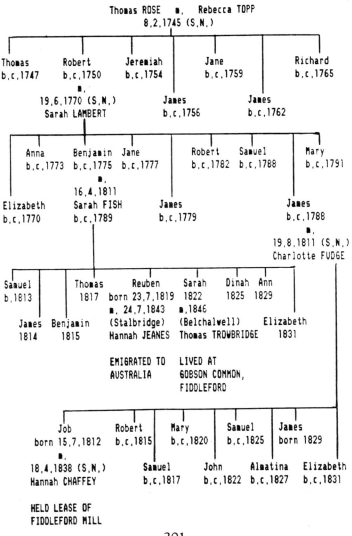

Fiddleford Mushrooms in Back Lane — 1992

Fiddleford Mushrooms, Banbury Cross — 1992

202

FIDDLEFORD IN 1992

When Where Elm Trees Grew was published in 1988, Fiddleford was described as "an inn, several farms and a tiny collection of old houses and cottages with three or four newer ones interspersed — a total of twenty-five properties". And so it is today. The lines by Thomas Hardy, quoted then, apply still:

"The people who lived here have left the spot,
And others are coming who knew them not"

though the houses change hands more frequently now than in 'the old days'.

Someone re-visiting the hamlet after an absence of four or five years is shocked to find that commerce has infiltrated the peaceful lanes and fields. Five very large polythene tunnels now stand in the old orchard belonging to The Paddock — essential for the mushroom farm, but an eyesore in the otherwise totally rural landscape. The heavy vehicles which service the business mutilate the verges and drains as they make their way to the site via the lane, far too narrow for them, which is the only access. However, such is the success of the venture that five more tunnels have recently been erected by the same firm at Banbury Cross — the end of Angers Lane — and it seems that even further expansion is contemplated.

Other recent changes are easier on the eye. Pond View has grown from a tiny bungalow into a sizeable house. The present owners have gone to great lengths to ensure that the extensions harmonise with the environment, and the result is an attractive building partially hidden from view by the old field hedge which has been allowed to grow higher, and which has been reinforced by a planting of conifers.

May Cottage was sold at the end of 1989, and the new occupants have chosen to allow it to 'disappear' behind a screen of trees and hedges. A brick extension with tiled roof has been erected at the north end of this listed building, the original part of which has pink-washed walls and a thatched roof.

Pond View — October 1992

May Cottage — October 1992

When Lester and Jane Wareham bought The Fiddleford Inn in December 1989 they immediately closed it for three months, during which time it underwent complete refurbishment. When it opened again in March 1990 the dining area had been enlarged and the emphasis was on the catering side of the business. Jane hopes that the cosy bar and pleasant restaurant, already becoming more popular with Fiddlefordians, will now establish itself as a 'local' for people living in the area.

Archway House (now The Fiddleford Inn)

The Fiddleford Inn — October 1992

The Fiddleford Inn — October 1992

Several of the other cottages are on the market or have been sold during the past four years. Fiddleford is still a charming place, though its character has changed in the comparatively short period since 1970. It has a more modern appearance. The majority of the residents are not locally born, and their work takes them away from the immediate area.

Gone are those days of twenty or thirty years ago when cows and sheep ambled through the lanes under the watchful eye of the farmers who lived there. There were then no large fields of cereals, and the hedges were never slashed by mechanical 'trimmers'. Animals grazed on the lush grass and the hedges were laid manually so that plants like 'old man's beard' flourished and gave pleasure to the local residents.

Memories evoke both pleasure and sadness. To indulge in nostalgia is perhaps to focus on a rose-coloured picture of what one chooses to remember! Having spent twenty very happy years in Fiddleford, however, I have come to the conclusion that I was fortunate indeed to have been there in 1970. The lazy North Dorset dialect was frequently heard, as some of the locally born farmers and cottagers still lived and worked in the gardens and fields. I remember with gratitude and affection "their own dear days".

Fiddleford·Mill·near·Sturminster·Newton

1891 CENSUS RETURNS

OKEFORD FITZPAINE (Entries for Fiddleford)

						Place of Birth
Gobson	COLLINS	James	widower	61	Carter/Farm Labourer	Belchalwell
"		Alice	daughter	19	Housekeeper for her father	Okef'd F'paine
"		Beatrice	grand-daughter	7	Scholar	" "

* * * * * * * * *

"	HAMES	Catherine	widow	62	Living on own means	Fifehead Neville
"		Frederick	son, single	25	Jobbing gardener	Sturminster
"		Catherine U.	daughter, single	21		Gobson, Okef'd F'paine
"		Gertrude A.	grand-daughter	10	Scholar	Dorchester

* * * * * * * * *

"	TROWBRIDGE	Thomas R.		31	Farmer	Child Okeford
"		Eliza Jane	wife	26		Sturminster
"		Maurice George	son	8 mths		Child Okeford

* * * * * * * * *

Angers	HARVEY	Henry Jas.		45	Farmer	Child Okeford
"		Sarah Jane	wife	41		Upton Noble

* * * * * * * * *

Fiddleford	WILDS	William	widower	69	Farmer	Marnhull
"		Alice M. M.	niece, single	19	Housekeeper	Fiddleford
"		Bessie J.	niece	13	General help	"

* * * * * * * * *

"	ADAMS	Philip C.		36	Farmer	Fiddleford
"		Sarah J.	wife	33		"
"		Emily	daughter	13		"
"		Philip C.	son	11		"
"		Ellen A.	daughter	8		"
"		Wilfred	son	5		"
"		Winnie	daughter	3		"
"		Colin	son	1		"

* * * * * * * * *

Fiddleford Railway Crossing	CORBIN	James		55	Railway platelayer	Knighton
"		Elizabeth	wife	36		Poole

209

CORBIN	Arthur A.	son	12	Scholar	Knighton
"	Sydney J.	son	10	"	East Pennard
"	Annie M.	daughter	8	"	Okef'd F'paine
"	Ethel B.	daughter	6	"	" "
"	Edwin T.	son	4		" "
"	Edith J.	daughter	2		" "

End of that part of the ecclesiastical parish of St. Nicholas, Child Okeford which is in the civil parish of Okeford Fitzpaine. This portion . . . . was added to Okeford Fitzpaine (Civil Parish) according to the provisions of the Divided Parishes Act.

Fiddleford Parish of Belchalwell	-RIDOUT	Job		75	Retired woodman (latterly he has become quite infirm . . .)	Sturminster
	"	Matilda	wife	73	Keeps house	Bishops Caundle
	CAINES	Ellen	grand-daughter	8	Scholar	Fiddleford

* * * * * * * * *

Fiddleford	MAIDMENT	Stephen		45	Coal merchant's laborer	Tarrant Rushton
"		Jane	wife	48	Keeps a small sweet shop	Hilton
"		Charles H.	son, single	20	Under-porter S. & D.R.	Shillingstone
"		Bessie F.	niece	8	Scholar	Bournemouth

* * * * * * * * *

Fiddleford	UPSHALL	James		41	Ag. Lab.	Bagber
"		Isabella	daughter, single	21	Glover	Sturminster
"		John	son, single	19	Gen. laborer	Fiddleford
"		Annie	daughter	11	Scholar	"
"		Rose	daughter	9	"	"
"		Charles	son	5	"	"
	ANDREWS	John	father-in-law	74	Widower, lives with son-in-law & receives Parish Relief	Not known has lost his memory entirely

* * * * * * * * *

	ADAMS	John		45	Ag. lab.	Fiddleford
	"	Martha	wife	42		Sturminster
	UPSHALL	Mary	mother-in-law	72	Widow. Kept partly by her son-in-law & assistance from Parish	"

* * * * * * * * *

	GODDARD	Henry		27	Ag. lab.	Fiddleford
	"	Harriet	wife	27		Portsmouth
	"	Henry	son	5	Scholar	Fiddleford
	"	Lucy	daughter	4		"
	"	Ellen	"	3		"
	"	Florence K.	"	1		"

* * * * * * * * * *

End of village of Okeford Fitzpaine which is in ecclesiastical parish of St. Michael.

Angers	POPE	Charles		27	Ag. Lab.	O'ford F'paine
	"	Lucy	wife	26		" " .
	"	Nellie L.	daughter	1		" "

* * * * * , * * * * *

Angers	THOMPSON	Herbert G.		29	Ag. Lab.	Wincanton
	"	Ann A.	wife	27		Dorset (N.K.)
	CHAMBERS	Lucy	daughter-in-law*	7	Scholar	Shillingstone
	THOMPSON	Walter T.	son	4		Fiddleford
	"	Kate E.	daughter	1		"

[* This must be an error]

* * * * * * * * * *

Fiddleford	FURNELL	George		49	Coal agent	Sutton Mandeville
	"	Elizabeth J.	wife	48	Grocer	Donhead

* * * * * * * * * *

	SAVORY	George		46	Gardener - dom. servant	Hammoon
	"	Louisa	wife	40		"

* * * * * * * * * *

	HORLOCK	Melinda	widow	70	In receipt of parochial relief	Shillingstone
	PITMAN	Maurice	grandson	12	Does odd jobs for fellmonger	Child Okeford
	"	Tom	"	7	Scholar	" "
	"	Bessie	grand-daughter	7	"	" "
	HORLOCK	George	son. single	27	Gen. laborer	" "

* * * * * * * * * *

	CRESSEY	Joseph		42	Carpenter	Fiddleford, O.F.
	"	Emma J.	wife	43		Marnhull
	"	Alice M.	daughter, single	18	Dressmaker	Fiddleford, O.F.
	"	Eva A.	"	8	Scholar	" "

211

| CRESSEY | *Lottie A. | daughter | 6 | Scholar | Fiddleford, O.F. |
| " | *Lottie R. | " | 4 | | " " |

[* This could be an error, as it is unlikely that two children would have the same name]

* * * * * * * * * *

CRESSEY	Stephen J.		28	Fellmonger, Hide Factor etc.	Fiddleford, O.F.
"	Rachael	wife	27		Bryanstone
"	Alan	son	5		Fiddleford, O.F.
"	Frederick	"	4		" "
"	Reginald	"	1		" "

* * * * * * * * * *

CAINES	Thomas		32	Jobbing mason	Hazelbury
"	Maria	wife	31		Sturminster
"	Ellen M.	daughter	10	Scholar	Fiddleford, O.F.
"	Walter T.	son	7	"	" "
"	Albert G.	"	5	"	" "
"	Frederick C.	"	2		" "
"	Edwin J.	"	1		" "

* * * * * * * * * *

HERRINGTON	Thomas		49	Dairyman	Woodyates, Cranbourne
"	Sarah	wife	50		Wilts, Bower Chalke
"	Herbert	son	20	Dairy laborer	Woodyates, Cranbourne

* * * * * * * * * *

DOUCH	George		25	Farm laborer	Hammoon
"	Charlotte	wife	26		Stur. Newton
"	Frederick G.	son	2		O'ford F'paine
"	Amy E.	daughter	7 mths		" "

* * * * * * * * * *

GODDARD	William		51	Ag. lab.	Sturminster
"	Mary A.	wife	49		Bagber
"	Agnes M.	daughter, single	22	Glover	Sturminster
"	Florence	" "	16	"	"
"	William J.	son	11	Scholar	Fiddleford

* * * * * * * * * *

GODDARD	Andrew		24	Ag. lab.	O'ford F'paine
"	Elizabeth	wife	24		Ansty
"	Sydney	son	2		Fiddleford
"	Infant in arms	"	1 mth		"
LEGG	Clement	Boarder, single	19	Gen. laborer	Wilts. Compton Chamberlayne

	SHORT	George			36	Ag. lab.	Sturminster
	"	Caroline	wife		42		"
		* * * * * * * * * *

	CHAMBERS	Alfred			34	Farm laborer	Child Okeford
	"	Maria	wife		24		Hinton St. Mary
	"	Louisa M.	daughter		2		Fiddleford O.F.
		* * * * * * * * * *

STURMINSTER NEWTON (Entries for Fiddleford)

Fiddleford	ROSE	Samuel			51	Farmer	Sturminster
The Mill	"	Mary	wife		49		"
	"	Harry	son, single	25	Farmer's son	"
	"	Arthur	" "	23	Relieving Officer	"
	"	Sidney	" "	21	Farmer's son	"
	"	Marion	daughter		19		"
	"	Frances	"		11		"
		* * * * * * * * * *

	GODDARD	Henry			27	Ag. lab.	Fiddleford
	"	Harriett	wife		27		Portsmouth
	"	Henry	son		5		Fiddleford
	"	Lucy	daughter		4		"
	"	Ellen	"		3		"
	"	Florence	"		1		"
		* * * * * * * * * *

	TOPP	Charles			58	Butcher	Sturminster
	"	Mary Ann	wife		61		"
	"	Mary Ann	daughter, single	20		"
	"	Eliza	" "	17		"
	"	Daniel	son		16		"
		* * * * * * * * * *

	ADAMS	George			83	Sub-Postm'ter	O'ford F'paine
	"	Jane	wife		59		Dorchester
		* * * * * * * * * *

Piddles Wood	SWAIN	John L.	widower		62	Gamekeeper (head)	Haselbury Bryan
	"	Catherine E.	daughter, single	20		Stur. Newton
		* * * * * * * * * *